SOCIAL ISSUES FIRSTHAND

The Holocaust

Other Books in the Social Issues Firsthand Series:

AIDS
Body Piercing and Tattoos
Bullying
Child Abuse and Neglect
Cults
Date and Acquaintance Rape
Disasters
Drunk Driving
Eating Disorders
Juvenile Crime
Prostitution
Sexual Predators
Teenage Pregnancy
Welfare

SOCIAL ISSUES FIRSTHAND

The Holocaust

Laurie Willis, Book Editor

GREENHAVEN PRESS
A part of Gale, Cengage Learning

GALE
CENGAGE Learning™

Detroit • New York • San Francisco • New Haven, Conn • Waterville, Maine • London

GALE
CENGAGE Learning

Christine Nasso, *Publisher*
Elizabeth Des Chenes, *Managing Editor*

© 2009 Greenhaven Press, a part of Gale, Cengage Learning.

Gale and Greenhaven Press are registered trademarks used herein under license.

For more information, contact:
Greenhaven Press
27500 Drake Rd.
Farmington Hills, MI 48331-3535
Or you can visit our Internet site at gale.cengage.com

ALL RIGHTS RESERVED.
No part of this work covered by the copyright herein may be reproduced, transmitted, stored, or used in any form or by any means graphic, electronic, or mechanical, including but not limited to photocopying, recording, scanning, digitizing, taping, Web distribution, information networks, or information storage and retrieval systems, except as permitted under Section 107 or 108 of the 1976 United States Copyright Act, without the prior written permission of the publisher.

For product information and technology assistance, contact us at

Gale Customer Support, 1-800-877-4253
For permission to use material from this text or product, submit all requests online at www.cengage.com/permissions

Further permissions questions can be emailed to permissionrequest@cengage.com

Articles in Greenhaven Press anthologies are often edited for length to meet page requirements. In addition, original titles of these works are changed to clearly present the main thesis and to explicitly indicate the author's opinion. Every effort is made to ensure that Greenhaven Press accurately reflects the original intent of the authors. Every effort has been made to trace the owners of copyrighted material.

Cover photograph reproduced by © Monsoon/Photolibrary/Corbis.

LIBRARY OF CONGRESS CATALOGING-IN-PUBLICATION DATA

The Holocaust / Laurie Willis, book editor.
    p. cm. -- (Social issues firsthand)
    Includes bibliographical references and index.
    ISBN 978-0-7377-4255-8 (hardcover)
    1. Holocaust, Jewish (1939-1945)--Juvenile literature. I. Willis, Laurie.
    D804.34.H645 2009
    940.53'18--dc22
                                                                            2008052821

Printed in the United States of America
1 2 3 4 5 6 7 13 12 11 10 09

Contents

Foreword   9

Introduction   12

Chapter 1: Ghettos and Concentration Camps

1. The First Days at Terezín   16
   Jana Renée Friesová
   A woman recalls her first few days after being forced to move into Terezín, a Czech ghetto, when she was a teenager.

2. A Smuggler in the Ghetto   23
   William J. Schiff, as told to Diane Plotkin
   A Jewish man talks about smuggling food and other items into the ghetto in Krakow, Poland, when he was a young man.

3. Arrival at Auschwitz   31
   Benny Grünfeld
   A Hungarian Jew remembers the horrors of his first day at Auschwitz, the notorious concentration camp and death camp, when he was a teenager.

4. Working in a Death Camp   38
   Leon Cohen, interviewed by Gideon Greif
   A Jew who was forced to work in the gas chambers in Auschwitz recalls the ordeals he faced.

Chapter 2: Life Outside the Camps

1. Working as a Spy   51
   Marthe Cohn, with Wendy Holden
   A French Jewish woman working as a spy in Germany describes relaying information about an ambush.

2. Forging Documents to Aid Jews   62
   Cioma Schönhaus
   A young graphic artist discovered that his talents could be used to forge documents to help Jews evade deportation from Germany.

3. Assisting with Deportations 66
Raymond-Raoul Lambert
A French Jewish man tells about having to assist with deportations of Jews while trying to save as many people as he could.

4. A Christian Tries to Help 70
Paul Zenon Wos, as told to Richard C. Lukas
A Polish Christian man helped Jews in the Warsaw ghetto until he too was taken to a concentration camp.

5. Belonging to the Hitler Youth Organization 78
Hubert Lutz, interviewed by Eric A. Johnson and Karl-Heinz Reuband
A German man talks about joining the Hitler Youth and about his wartime memories.

Chapter 3: Liberation

1. Leaving Auschwitz 89
Agi Rubin and Henry Greenspan
A woman prisoner's journal entries describe her journey to freedom.

2. Freedom Arrives at Oberaltstadt 97
Helen Freeman, as told to Joseph Freeman
A Jewish woman in a Polish concentration camp recalls what happened when Russian and American troops arrived to liberate them.

3. The Trials at Nuremberg 106
Richard W. Sonnenfeldt
An American soldier who acted as an interpreter during the war crimes trials in Nuremberg relates his experience interviewing Nazi leader Hermann Göring.

Chapter 4: Lasting Effects of the Holocaust

1. Hitler Killed My Father 118
Shirley Paryzer Levy
A child of a Holocaust survivor asserts that the effects of the Holocaust stayed with her father for the remainder of his life.

2. Lessons to Be Learned from the Holocaust **121**
Anthony Lipmann
At the time of the 60th anniversary of liberation of the concentration camps, a man reflects on his mother's and grandmother's experiences in the camps and asserts that Jews must help to free the world from hate.

3. A Visit to Auschwitz **127**
Natalie Semotiuk
A contemporary teen recounts the feelings she experienced during a visit to Auschwitz.

Organizations to Contact **129**

For Further Research **136**

Index **139**

Foreword

Social issues are often viewed in abstract terms. Pressing challenges such as poverty, homelessness, and addiction are viewed as problems to be defined and solved. Politicians, social scientists, and other experts engage in debates about the extent of the problems, their causes, and how best to remedy them. Often overlooked in these discussions is the human dimension of the issue. Behind every policy debate over poverty, homelessness, and substance abuse, for example, are real people struggling to make ends meet, to survive life on the streets, and to overcome addiction to drugs and alcohol. Their stories are ubiquitous and compelling. They are the stories of everyday people—perhaps your own family members or friends—and yet they rarely influence the debates taking place in state capitols, the national Congress, or the courts.

The disparity between the public debate and private experience of social issues is well illustrated by looking at the topic of poverty. Each year the U.S. Census Bureau establishes a poverty threshold. A household with an income below the threshold is defined as poor, while a household with an income above the threshold is considered able to live on a basic subsistence level. For example, in 2003 a family of two was considered poor if its income was less than $12,015; a family of four was defined as poor if its income was less than $18,810. Based on this system, the bureau estimates that 35.9 million Americans (12.5 percent of the population) lived below the poverty line in 2003, including 12.9 million children below the age of eighteen.

Commentators disagree about what these statistics mean. Social activists insist that the huge number of officially poor Americans translates into human suffering. Even many families that have incomes above the threshold, they maintain, are likely to be struggling to get by. Other commentators insist that the statistics exaggerate the problem of poverty in the United States. Compared to people in developing countries, they point out, most so-called poor families have a high quality of life. As stated by journalist Fidelis Iyebote, "Cars are owned by 70 percent of 'poor' households. . . . Color televisions belong to 97 percent of the 'poor' [and] videocassette recorders belong to nearly 75 percent. . . . Sixty-four percent have microwave ovens, half own a stereo system, and over a quarter possess an automatic dishwasher."

However, this debate over the poverty threshold and what it means is likely irrelevant to a person living in poverty. Simply put, poor people do not need the government to tell them whether they are poor. They can see it in the stack of bills they cannot pay. They are aware of it when they are forced to choose between paying rent or buying food for their children. They become painfully conscious of it when they lose their homes and are forced to live in their cars or on the streets. Indeed, the written stories of poor people define the meaning of poverty more vividly than a government bureaucracy could ever hope to. Narratives composed by the poor describe losing jobs due to injury or mental illness, depict horrific tales of childhood abuse and spousal violence, recount the loss of friends and family members. They evoke the slipping away of social supports and government assistance, the descent into substance abuse and addiction, the harsh realities of life on the streets. These are the perspectives on poverty that are too often omitted from discussions over the extent of the problem and how to solve it.

Greenhaven Press's *Social Issues Firsthand* series provides a forum for the often-overlooked human perspectives on society's most divisive topics of debate. Each volume focuses on one social issue and presents a collection of ten to sixteen narratives by those who have had personal involvement with the topic. Extra care has been taken to include a diverse range of perspectives. For example, in the volume on adoption,

Foreword

readers will find the stories of birth parents who have made an adoption plan, adoptive parents, and adoptees themselves. After exposure to these varied points of view, the reader will have a clearer understanding that adoption is an intense, emotional experience full of joyous highs and painful lows for all concerned.

The debate surrounding embryonic stem cell research illustrates the moral and ethical pressure that the public brings to bear on the scientific community. However, while nonexperts often criticize scientists for not considering the potential negative impact of their work, ironically the public's reaction against such discoveries can produce harmful results as well. For example, although the outcry against embryonic stem cell research in the United States has resulted in fewer embryos being destroyed, those with Parkinson's, such as actor Michael J. Fox, have argued that prohibiting the development of new stem cell lines ultimately will prevent a timely cure for the disease that is killing Fox and thousands of others.

Each book in the series contains several features that enhance its usefulness, including an in-depth introduction, an annotated table of contents, bibliographies for further research, a list of organizations to contact, and a thorough index. These elements—combined with the poignant voices of people touched by tragedy and triumph—make the Social Issues Firsthand series a valuable resource for research on today's topics of political discussion.

Introduction

The Holocaust was the systematic extermination of approximately six million Jews by the National Socialist German Workers' Party (Nazis) under the leadership of Adolf Hitler during World War II. The word "Holocaust" is from the Greek, meaning "sacrifice by fire." Some people prefer to use the Hebrew term "Shoah," meaning "calamity." The Nazis believed that they belonged to a superior race, epitomized by blue-eyed, blond Caucasians. They claimed that Jews were inferior and that their existence was a threat to the purity of the Nazi race. The Roma (Gypsies), millions of Slavic people (Poles and Russians), people with disabilities, homosexuals, Jehovah's Witnesses, Communists, Socialists, and others were also persecuted by the Nazis. Some people use the word "Holocaust" to refer exclusively to the genocide of the Jews; others use the term more broadly to include all people who were persecuted or killed by the Nazis.

When the Nazis came to power in 1933, more than nine million Jews were living in Europe. By the end of World War II in 1945, nearly two-thirds of them had died in what the Nazis called the "Final Solution of the Jewish Question"—the plan to murder all European Jews. In many of the countries invaded by Germany during World War II, the Nazis forced Jews to leave their homes and live in overcrowded neighborhoods called ghettos. Some ghettos were enclosed and guarded like prisons; in other ghettos, movements of the residents outside the ghetto were allowed but very restricted. Most had no opportunity to earn money, and they had little to eat or drink. Many Jews were taken from the ghettos or directly from their homes and deported to concentration camps, where they were imprisoned. Stripped of their belongings, humiliated and dehumanized, they were housed in barracks with hundreds of other prisoners, in rows of bunk beds stacked to the ceiling.

Introduction

The barracks were unheated, unsanitary, and crowded, and there was very little food or water. Many people died of disease, malnutrition, and starvation. Some were used as slave labor until they were no longer able to work. Others were herded in large groups into gas chambers disguised as showers, forced to undress, and killed with poisonous gas. Some were shot and piled into pits full of corpses.

Near the end of the war, as the German military collapsed, soldiers from the Allied forces (the United States, Great Britain, the Soviet Union, and others) began to liberate the camp inmates as they encountered them. After the war, Jews lived in camps for displaced persons before emigrating to Israel, the United States, and other countries.

By the late twentieth and early twenty-first centuries, most of those who lived through the Holocaust had reached old age, and many felt an urgency to record their experiences. Numerous memoirs have been written, in part to ensure that the stories are told and the horrors are not forgotten. In his book *Reflections on the Holocaust*, Elie Wiesel, Holocaust survivor and author of more than forty books on the subject, says:

> The man writing these lines must be frank: he doesn't want to tell you about this uniquely bloody and murderous period; he's reluctant to talk about his past. What can he achieve by making you sad? Why keep denouncing the indifference of some and the collaboration of others? And why bring up his own past when millions of other human beings have suffered as much as—if not more than—he has?
>
> And yet ... the survivor must be a witness.

As the well-known quote by George Santayana says, "Those who cannot remember the past are condemned to repeat it." Many of those whose stories are included in this book have spoken of how difficult it is to tell of their own painful past and yet how important it is to do so.

For the same reason, some of the concentration camps have been converted today into museums where the lives of those who died in the camps can be reconstructed and memorialized. The need to remember the events of the Holocaust is so compelling that museums have been erected around the world, far from the locations where the actual events of the Holocaust took place. In the United States, there is a national Holocaust Memorial Museum in Washington, D.C., and others are spread across the country.

This book contains viewpoints of people who experienced the Holocaust. Some of them survived to tell their stories. Others kept diaries that were made public and published many years after they died in the camps. The first chapter contains accounts of what life was like in the ghettos and concentration camps. The second chapter includes depictions of life outside the camps from the point of view of those who escaped or avoided capture, and of those who worked to aid and protect the Jewish people. The time of liberation is described in the third chapter. In the final chapter, members of later generations discuss the impact the events of the Holocaust have had on their lives.

SOCIAL ISSUES
FIRSTHAND

CHAPTER 1

Ghettos and
Concentration Camps

The First Days at Terezín

Jana Renée Friesová

Before being forced to move to the ghetto at Terezín, Jana Renée Friesová had lived a comfortable life in Czechoslovakia. In this excerpt from her book, Fortress of My Youth: Memoir of a Terezín Survivor, *she recalls her family's first days in the Terezín ghetto and concentration camp. First, they were herded into a large, crowded barn-like building, where there was barely room to sit down. When she wanted to use the latrine, she discovered that there was only a trench dug into the earth, with planks nailed above it. There were no walls or doors—no privacy at all. This circumstance seemed like the ultimate indignity to her, until a few days later when she saw her first corpses, piled haphazardly onto a cart that was pulled by human beings.*

Until December 1942, I had not the faintest knowledge of ghetto conditions. Now about 60,000 people were packed into Terezín. Even in the war years, pre-Christmas days had been full of poetry and goodwill. Now, from one day to the next, this was replaced with anxiety about the unknown, and disgust with filth and the total loss of privacy.

The first step: Bohušovice station platform. The SS dogs, searchlights in the darkening evening. Shouting. Hundreds of men, women and children somehow hung onto their bundles and cases and lined up for the march from Bohušovice to Terezín. Confused and frightened, we suddenly heard a muffled call. "Fries family. Is the family Fries from Josefov here?"

We turned towards the sound of the voice. It belonged to a tall young man wearing a quilted work jacket. My parents knew him. It was Milan, the twenty-five-year-old son of a

Jana Renée Friesová, *Fortress of My Youth: Memoir of a Terezín Survivor*. Madison: The University of Wisconsin Press, 2002. Copyright © 2002 by the Board of Regents of the University of Wisconsin System. Reproduced by permission.

wealthy family from Jaroměř. At that moment he seemed to us like an angel from heaven. In a flash he joined this strange, sad procession and, without any explanation, gave us orders: "Put all your belongings aside and move on. I will look after your baggage. You will get everything back after you have gone through the entry procedures into the ghetto. Nothing will be lost, don't worry."

It was a miracle. How glad we were to get rid of those burdensome kilograms. How gladly we gave way to the feeling that we were not altogether nameless, that someone knew about us, someone had looked after us.

Arrival at the "Floodgate"

In the damp darkness, we dragged ourselves into an even darker town. We went through the town gates and along the streets to the barracks which was the destination of all new transports. Worn out, shivering and hunched up with cold, we found ourselves in a badly lit room. There were tables all around, the SS behind them rummaging through people's belongings and confiscating whatever they liked. But our guardian angel appeared—how did he find us? He turned to Father, Mother and me and whispered, "Come with me." We made our way through the crowd after him.

"Here is all your baggage, nothing is missing, nobody went through it. Take it and go up there to the first floor. I cannot come with you. When it's possible, I will find you. I still have a few people to help." He disappeared.

Even now, I can recall the dreamy state of those first few hours that night and the following day. It was as if it did not concern me—it could not be me, or my elegant mother or my kind father walking up a slippery ramp into a huge space, which was probably a stable. Occasionally we tripped across wooden ridges which divided up the ramp. These ridges were helpful. They prevented us from slipping under the weight of our bags. There was a dirty, yellow-brown liquid trickling beneath our feet. It was only later that we realised what had been flowing under us, and had frozen here and there. Urine, human excrement from people who were too weak and sick to get up from their straw mattresses and go to the latrines in the middle of the barracks courtyard.

Packed into a Large Room

Our "angel" was gone. He disappeared as quickly and unobtrusively as he had appeared. He would locate us again but only after several weeks. Right now we almost collapsed under the weight of our bags and Father and I tried to lighten Mother's load. Finally, at the top of the ramp we entered a vast, endless area. There was no room to move. All around, people were lying down or sitting among their bags and suitcases. The day before our arrival, a transport had come from Mladá Boleslav and had not as yet been processed. Into this chaos hundreds and hundreds of others had arrived. No space was made for us, nor for those who had accompanied us, and no one was prepared to share their mattress. We were looked upon as intruders by those who had arrived earlier, though at the same time they were actually glad to see us. As "established residents" they already knew that one or other of the transports would have to go east.

Someone said, "Don't make yourselves too comfortable, you are probably moving on. We have been here for a while, we haven't unpacked, why would they send us?" Mladá Boleslavians used a kind of logical argument where logic did not exist.

Only a few naked globes lit up that whole space. From among those in our transport a few of us remained standing. The others eventually found a spot to lodge themselves, surrounded by a herd of "permanent" inhabitants. In spite of their arriving only a few hours ahead of us, they eagerly asked for the news from the front. They were glad that the Russians were advancing and that the war would end soon. Even after that, nobody moved an inch, and we stood and stood until I felt my legs almost give way.

Ghettos and Concentration Camps

Again a guardian angel was looking over us and nudged someone whom we knew from the distant past, well before the war years. He took pity on us and suggested we sit next to him on his mattress. What a relief to sit down on the bare mattress, our bags around us. Were we saying to ourselves that this could not last very long, that it made no sense to confine us here unproductively? Perhaps it also occurred to us to wonder how long we could last in this unventilated but icy room. I can remember how I worried about where and how I would change my clothes and wash for the night. How trivial! Gradually, people separated into different groups and the talking went on and on ... speculation, complaints and even astonishment about what was happening.

I have no idea how we survived that first night. The next day, a trickle of people from the ghetto came to see us: acquaintances, relatives and even strangers. Some had been here for ages—well, a month, half a year, some even for a year. After the first greetings and embraces, we, the new ones, could feel some animosity from the ghetto dwellers. It took a while before we realised this. Why, even my Aunt Olga, my grandmother's sister who always loved me and I her, was different somehow. She was strange. Slowly, and in a roundabout way, barely perceptible accusations emerged: how well-off we apparently were; we had had weeks, even months, longer of sleeping in our own beds; how well we looked, we probably lacked nothing; we had brought food supplies; and we were wearing good quality, intact clothes. They had already eaten their supplies, unlike us. We felt embarrassed in front of them. I can vividly recall that feeling of embarrassment. A greying, unsightly old woman with thin hair, whom no one knew, loudly reproached us, insisting that the arrival of a new transport meant that the previous ones would go east. There was no one else to whom they could shout, whisper or otherwise express the anxiety and fear which had overcome them.

The Latrine Without Walls

Some time towards morning I had to get up from the mattress, that puny bit of security, and look for a place where I could carry out a primitive human need. The old and the sick could not manage that, and hence the sludge that had trickled under our feet when we arrived. I had to look for a different solution. I found out that the latrines were in the courtyard. The courtyard was large, square and very clean. The building in which we were interned seemed to be part of the barracks complex, and occasionally people appeared in its "welcoming" portico. I saw the latrine immediately. It was in the middle of this tidy courtyard—a rectangular trench with roughly nailed planks above it. No walls, no doors. Several people could sit there at any one time. The courtyard appeared deserted but recent experiences had not changed me to such an extent that I could cope with the possibility of somebody watching me during this private function. I panicked. What now? I could not tolerate this, it was beyond belief. I had to solve this situation now, without delay. I told myself that I would try to sneak into the forbidden buildings which housed the elderly ghetto residents. People lived there who had surely endured the same horrors as we had. Up a few steps, on the first floor, was a sign: *Eintritt Verboten*, Entry Forbidden. Past the sign were the sought-after doors. How grateful I was. I realised that a person does not have to abide by every order. Probably those older than I would not risk anything, would not look for an alternative; they would rather suffer the humiliation of the latrine in the courtyard.

Quietly, I opened the door and I was overwhelmed by the damp and the smell of disinfectant. How pleasant. I hurried, but noticed that an old lady, all skin and bone although neatly dressed in black, was sitting at the rear of quite a large room. I hid my number CH 18 under my jumper. In spite of this, my plump cheeks and good clothing made her realise that I was a newcomer. She screamed piercingly at me. Even though

I did not understand her German (much later on, I began to distinguish the Berlin from the Viennese accent), I well understood her tone and gestures. She wanted to throw me out. In my poor German, I explained and I flattered her—how clean she kept the toilet, using disinfectant, and what it meant to me not to have to go to the latrine. The old woman came and stood in front of the toilet door and indicated quite clearly to me that if I did not leave, she would make a scene. And she, a Jewess, threw me, also a Jewess and similarly afflicted, out. Still in a state of shock, I slinked over to the latrine in the middle of the courtyard. No one was about. Lucky me.

Moving into the Ghetto

I do not remember if two or three days passed before they moved us from the "floodgate". My parents went to look for acquaintances and relatives whose ghetto addresses we knew before we left home, when we had sent them the permitted half-kilogram parcels. Father and Mother wanted to find someone who could advise us how to procure our own mattresses in the barracks or houses to give us a base, a feeling of identity and also an address to which my grandfather and grandmother could write.

In that December, the ghetto was bursting at its seams. Every day, other transports arrived from various districts in Bohemia and Moravia. Nobody worried about housing people. The Germans did not care how the Jewish Council tackled this insoluble problem. The Council was almost powerless. Bewildered, cold and sad after the experience of the floodgate, we wandered about the ghetto and looked for help. My parents and I had worked out some meeting points if we found accommodation. If this failed, Father had decided to seek out his brother Josef whom he knew was the *Hausälteste*, administrator, in one of the houses.

Before we found this uncle, I roamed around the streets aimlessly. The narrow, straight streets of the former Terezín fortress were unbelievably overcrowded. Was everyone hurrying somewhere? While still at home, I used to have nightmares from which I awoke terrified, but no nightmare was as terrible as this reality. I wonder why I was not overpowered by fear, but rather by curiosity? What would come next, what could happen to me? It even occurred to me that perhaps it would be the re-emergence of our guardian angel, the young man who had led us through our first predicament here.

More significantly, that day, I saw a cart pulled by human beings. I pushed my way through the throng. I saw a two-wheeled cart on which was a messy heap of things resembling bodies. Unfortunately I did not believe my first impression, and without thinking what I was doing I stepped closer. Yes, they were bodies, stiff and unreal, thrown here and there, legs and arms dangling from the cart. The cart-pullers occasionally stopped to straighten up the load. When I realised that I was not mistaken, I became rigid. I could not move. People bumped into me. Until that moment I had never seen a corpse. And now this.

The anguished realisation that a human being can have so little worth was the revelation of my first day in the ghetto. Later, nothing, or almost nothing, was as horrifying.

A Smuggler in the Ghetto

William J. Schiff, as told to Diane Plotkin

William J. Schiff was twenty years old when his family was forced to move to the Jewish ghetto in Kraków, Poland. His father was forced to leave his job and became demoralized in the ghetto because he was not able to work or support his family. As the oldest boy in the family, Schiff took responsibility for finding and providing food. There was very little food inside the ghetto. He bribed the guards so that he would be able to leave the ghetto. Once outside, he went to the market to get food. Because Polish money was worthless, he traded items of value from his family's home. His mother helped him design a coat with inside pockets so that he could smuggle the food and other items back into the ghetto.

At the beginning of the war, I was exactly twenty years old. There were five people in my family: my mother, father, sister, brother, and myself. There were about one and one-half years difference in age between the siblings. I was the eldest. My sister was the only girl. She was a smart girl but spoiled. My younger brother was just an average guy but scared like everyone else. All three of us were practically grown up when the war began.

After the Germans occupied the country, the Polish police took over in Kraków. They were just like the Germans; they did exactly what the Germans told them and were happy to do it. The ghetto was formed in 1941. It was a small ghetto. From north to south, it contained about seven streets; from east to west there were about four or five. They built brick walls around it so we couldn't escape. There were three main

William J. Schiff, as told to Diane Plotkin, *Life in the Ghettos During the Holocaust*. Syracuse: Syracuse University Press, 2005. Copyright © 2005 by Syracuse University Press. All rights reserved. Reproduced by permission.

gates with Polish police guarding them. Unless you had a pass, there was no way out. I had one, but no one else in my family did.

My family was living in Kazimiercz, the Jewish section of town, but the Germans took a section of Kraków called Podgorze, which was not near the downtown, and started moving Jews there. I was the one who found an apartment in the ghetto for my family. I don't remember the size, but there were two rooms: a kitchen and a bedroom. The kitchen was used for cooking, dining, and everything else.

When they moved us to the ghetto, I was dating Rosalie, who was sixteen at the time. At first, they also allowed some of the Jews from Kraków to move to small towns nearby. She had been living in a nice apartment near the Vistula River and moved to one of these small towns with her mother, brother, and sister in 1941. Her father had run away in 1931 and was never allowed to return to his family. I helped Rosalie's family move out of Kraków. After that, I used to buy off the policeman and leave the ghetto to visit her once or twice a week. My parents didn't know because usually if you were found leaving the ghetto, you could be killed. A Polish policeman or a German would just take you away and shoot you.

There was no work in the ghetto, no way to make a living. My daddy had been a barber and a beautician before the war, but when we moved into the ghetto, he had to sign his shop over to the employee who had worked for him the longest. Now it seemed like my daddy was my child, and I was the father. He just cried all day.

Smuggling to Take Care of His Family

The Germans didn't give us any rations, so we had nothing to eat at all. People were dying on the streets, so somebody was going to have to provide for the family, and I was the guy. We were also concerned about Rosalie's family. Her mother had two sisters, but they had their own problems. When I would see a person lying on the street, I wanted to pick him up and help him, but I had a family of five to feed. I had to worry about my parents. If I didn't take care of my family, no one else would. Human beings are not selfish, just concerned with their own self-preservation.

Many people used to smuggle different things into the ghetto. For instance, there was a baker making bread, and somebody smuggled flour into the ghetto for it. I didn't know how they did it, but some of us had connections with the Poles outside, so I started to buy my way out, too. The second week after I started, I noticed that there was a market close to where Rosalie lived. When I came home, I told my mother about it, and when I told her how I was buying my way out of the ghetto, she got hysterical. I also told her about Rosalie's family, and she said we had to do something to help them or they would die. Then she went with me to visit them and also look at the market. We decided that when I went to visit Rosalie, I would stop at the market and try to buy something. You couldn't buy anything for money because Polish money didn't have any value, so I would take whatever was of value in the house and trade it for food. Rosalie's mother gave me some valuables, too, so I could buy them some food, but they didn't have much left.

A Special Coat for Smuggling

My mother and I talked about the best way to smuggle. Subsequently, I would go to the market wearing a ragged jacket and ragged pants with holes in them. On top of this, I wore a heavy coat that was too big for me. It wasn't exactly black but was very dark. I didn't put my arms in it but wore it like a cape, draped over my hands and arms. Then, like an old man, I covered my head with it. I could wear this all summer, too, because it didn't get too hot, only seventy-eight or eighty degrees. I also put a large belt around my waist.

I would go to the market and trade whatever valuables we had for chickens, but I had no idea of what kind of chickens to buy. Because the Jewish people wouldn't eat chickens if they weren't kosher, I had to bring them into the ghetto alive. For me to do that, my mother sewed a little sack of white cloth, like a pillowcase with holes in it. There was enough space inside each one for me to put a live chicken, hang the bag over my belt, and clip it on with two pins. I would buy four chickens at a time and put two on each side and two in back, under my coat. What was considered good at that time was the chicken fat, so fat chickens were very expensive. If they weren't fat, nobody would touch them, and no woman could sell them. My mother also sewed pockets inside my coat so I could smuggle some fruit and sometimes a little bit of butter.

Sometimes I took my brother with me. He was scared and couldn't make decisions, but he followed me blindly. I used to bring him to the gate, find a spot in some Gentile person's house, and leave him there. Then I took the clothes I used for smuggling and went to make sure there was a policeman I knew at the gate. Before I left the ghetto, the first thing I had to do was hand the policeman money to buy him off. I would give him as much money as he asked for and tell him what time I would be back. Sometimes when I came, the policeman wasn't there, so I just took a chance and walked out. I would go out two or three times a week, and I always got away with it.

I went out like this for seven months. Going to the market took, on the average, about two and one-half or three hours to walk there, then four or five hours heading back. I usually got there by about noon. One day I left about seven or eight o'clock in the morning. When I got there, the market hadn't opened yet. It wasn't until about one or two o'clock before I could start my buying, so by the time I came back to the ghetto, it was almost five o'clock. While I was gone for so long, my mother had cried and was eating her heart out be-

Ghettos and Concentration Camps

cause she had let me go. Almost every time I left and came back, Rosalie was waiting at the gate with my mother, and she was there that day, too.

Helping Other People

People started to notice that I had connections and was bringing food into the ghetto. I began to need some help and found some other people. This way I didn't have to go out three times a week, maybe once or twice. Almost every morning somebody came to my house and wanted me to go out, but they didn't have the money to buy enough to eat. My mother was soft-hearted. If somebody was a good Jew, she would give the food to them for less than what I had paid for it, and I would get mad. She said to me, "You have to have a heart. You must understand how things are for people." I used to argue with her because when I had a bad day, nobody had mercy on me. I also had arguments with my sister about it. Because she was the only girl, my mother said she was right and always agreed with her. One time I got mad at my mother and told her that I was the one who risked my life, but she was the one who told me what to do. The next time I started to go out, she didn't say a word, so I just left. But I gave in later because I loved my mother, and the smuggling went on.

At the beginning of 1942, all Jews outside Kraków were ordered to move into the ghetto; they had two or three days to do it. When Rosalie moved, I went to the same gate to find the policeman I knew because he was the one who let me out. Each time you did this, you took a chance. You had to pick the right one, and I was lucky each time. When my family had to come into the ghetto, we had been living close to the apartment we moved into, but Rosalie's family had to move several miles away. It was a long distance because we didn't even have bicycles. After the war broke out, the police had confiscated them for the Polish army. We also had no means of communication.

The Holocaust

I found them one big room because everything else was taken. I don't think the room even had a window, just a door with a window in it. I don't remember exactly where it was, but it was not far from me, just four or five blocks. I went to their apartment in the small town and moved the whole family to the ghetto, although legally, I wasn't allowed to. They brought bags with all their clothes and whatever else was left from their home, such as a few dishes. I gave her mother money to get settled in, but she refused. She was wondering where I got it. After Rosalie came to the ghetto, we were together all day.

Getting Married in the Ghetto

The Germans started to reduce the ghetto population, and on June 1, 1942, they evacuated my family. My parents didn't have identity papers, but I did. I didn't want my mother to go because I loved her dearly. She was the smart one in the family. After that, my sister and I were the only ones left. On June 8, 1942, they arrested Rosalie's mother, sister, and brother. If Rosalie hadn't known me, she would have been arrested, too. Her mother trusted me and gave me an ultimatum. She said, "First, you have to marry her. I trust you, and don't touch her until you marry." She [Rosalie] was just nineteen. Her mother had sewn gold coins into Rosalie's coat, but I wouldn't take them. I said, "Don't worry about it." After that, it was hard to get out of the ghetto.

We had few witnesses at our wedding because they had taken our parents. We were first married by a rabbi and then through the Polish court. I think an official came to the ghetto and gave us legal papers. Many Jews at this time refused to be married by government officials. They didn't recognize court marriages, so according to Jewish law we weren't legally married. The Polish court didn't recognize rabbinical marriages because according to them a rabbi was just like any other person. But the majority of Jews, like my parents, were more modern and open-minded.

After my parents and Rosalie's family were taken, my sister, Rosalie, and I were left in two rooms. Before we were married, I had moved Rosalie into the bedroom with my sister while I slept in the kitchen. After I married Rosalie, I moved into the bedroom with her, and my sister slept in the kitchen.

Smuggling Metal

After I married Rosalie, I found another way to smuggle. The Germans sent me to work in a nail factory. They would pick me up every morning and take me there. In charge was a Pole who worked for the *Wehrmacht* [the German armed forces]. Our labor group consisted of about twenty or twenty-two boys. The oldest one was twenty-seven, and the youngest was nineteen. The oldest was in charge. I was second oldest, so I was next. Anytime there was trouble, I could get out of it because I was close to him.

I noticed that there were stacks of aluminum in a warehouse, just like pieces of aluminum pipe. The Germans kept them in this storage shed; they had stolen them from the Jews. One of the boys who worked in the factory was stealing these, but I couldn't because I worked outside with the other boys. I decided I could be his partner; I could smuggle them out. Because he was good at stealing, he brought me four or five pieces every day. They were about a half or a full foot wide and about two feet long. I had six or seven at one time and tied them together with my jacket. Then I would give them to my partner, and he would sell them. I don't know who he sold them to. He wouldn't tell me because he was afraid that I would take his business away from him. He had some connections with Jews in the ghetto who had associations with Poles who made a living selling these on the black market. I watched how much money he was selling them for, and he paid me out of that.

I started taking them to sell in the ghetto, too. If I could sell them, I could buy clothes for my sister and Rosalie and get some food. One day the guard suspected me of bringing them into the ghetto and arrested me. He checked me over from top to bottom. I had put the pieces in my right back pocket. Although he checked me from my feet up and in my left back side, he never checked me on the right and let me go. Amon Goeth, the commandant of Plaszow [a concentration camp], was there but didn't say anything. I wonder how I got away with it. Just plain luck!

We were forced to leave the ghetto and walk to Plaszow in October 1942. On September 19, 1943, when I came back from work, I found out that they had taken Rosalie to Skarzsysko [a labor camp]. My whole world collapsed. I jumped on everybody; I didn't care who. I even jumped on two Germans in uniform, but they didn't shoot me. Two boys tried to help me, but the Nazis shot them. Me, they just hit on the head with a gun. If they didn't shoot me then, they would never shoot me. After that, I jumped on a train, thinking it was going in the same direction, but I wound up in [the concentration camp] Auschwitz and continued my smuggling there. I never got caught for it, either in the ghetto or in Auschwitz.

Arrival at Auschwitz

Benny Grünfeld

In this excerpt from his book, A Teenager in Hitler's Death Camps, *Benny Grünfeld describes his first days at the concentration camp and death camp Auschwitz, the horror he saw there, and his own luck that kept him alive. Grünfeld's whole family was transported to Auschwitz when he was a teenager. Upon arrival, they were separated by gender and he never saw his mother again. The men and boys were sorted into groups. They did not know it at the time, but Grünfeld and his brother Herman were in the group that was allowed to live. His father and his other brother were destined for the gas chamber. At a second sorting, Grünfeld did not want to be separated from Herman, so he snuck into his brother's group. As it turned out, he was again destined to avoid the gas chamber.*

After we had been confined to the freight car for four days and nights, the doors finally opened. The sun was just rising, and we encountered a nightmarish scene: live barbed-wire fences, inmates in striped uniforms, armed guards with German shepherds. We had come to the Auschwitz-Birkenau extermination camp in Poland.

Even before getting off the train, we heard shrill, impatient shouts: "Women and children over here!" "Men all together!" Command after command. Suddenly my mother was separated from us. It all happened in the bat of an eyelash. Then she was gone. We didn't even have time to say good-bye. She vanished, whisked away by the guards—and I was never to see her again.

Benny Grünfeld, *A Teenager in Hitler's Death Camps*. Dallas, TX: BenBella Books, Inc., 2007. Copyright © 1995 by Benny Grünfeld, Magnus Henrekson and Olle Hager. Revision copyright © 2006 by Benny Grünfeld, Magnus Henrekson and Olle Hager. Reproduced by permission.

Sorted for the Gas Chamber

They led my father, my two brothers, and me to a courteous, uniformed doctor. Pointing to me and to my younger brother Alexander, he asked if we were twins. My father, who spoke German, answered truthfully that Alexander was thirteen and that I had just turned sixteen. The doctor then gestured that I was to go to the right, Alexander to the left. My brother Herman was directed to the right, my father to the left.

Herman and I to the right. My father and Alexander to the left. It was all decided right then and there. Going to the left meant the gas chamber.

An inmate led us into the camp. Torah scrolls were scattered along the road. Cold shivers ran down my spine when I saw our most holy scripture, so sacred that it may not be touched by human hands, lying like rubbish in the mud and filth. Instinctively, I bent down and picked up a little prayer book, which was to be my constant companion and consolation from that time on. I decided to hide it in one of my shoes, and since it was so tiny, there was actually room for it there.

After being taken to a large barn, we were ordered to undress, except for our shoes and waist belt. Next a group of inmates gave us crew cuts and cut off all our bodily hair. The scissors were blunt, and it hurt when they yanked on the hair. When they were through, they took us to another building, where they smeared us with a corrosive liquid disinfectant. Although we showered immediately afterwards, our skin smarted for several days. The building that housed the showers was located close to the crematorium.

There was a picket fence in the back of the building. Through the chinks we could see a steam shovel digging enormous pits. Later we discovered that the Germans burned bodies in the pits.

However, the crematorium didn't have the capacity to burn the bodies of all the Jews who arrived each day from Hungary and other parts of Europe to be gassed to death.

Death Pits

At that time, the summer of 1944, more people were killed daily in Auschwitz-Birkenau than ever before. The pits were the worst fate a Jew could suffer. One by one they were brought forward, shot in the back of the head with a small-bore revolver and slung into the fiery pit while still struggling for life. Occasionally the SS officers threw a child into the pit without even shooting him. Smoke from the crematorium and the pits constantly wafted through the camp. We were plagued day and night by the nauseating odor of burning flesh. We had obviously come to hell on Earth.

When we were finished showering, they led us to an area called C Camp. Birkenau was surrounded on all sides by a live barbed-wire fence. On the other side of the fence were deep ditches and watch-towers with armed sentries.

Our barrack in C Camp was one of hundreds of virtually identical wooden buildings, each of which could house approximately a thousand inmates. Instead of beds, we had rectangular cots, stacked three high. Ten people lying back to back could fit in one cot. But if one person wanted to turn around, everyone else had to do so at the same time. There wasn't even straw to lie on, only rough planks. The people on the bottom cot had the worst time of it, since they lay directly on the ground.

The Inmate Hierarchy

Within the camp itself, everything was run by inmates. The SS officers entered the camp only for executions, inspections, and body searches when we returned from work in the evenings. A frightful kind of egoism was the rule, and the privileged inmates were extraordinarily brutal toward us ordinary inmates.

The Holocaust

The highest posts were reserved for German criminals, Aryans, "ethnic Germans" (who had been living in other countries), Polish Christians, etc. On the next rung down in the hierarchy were the assistants, who could be of any one of several nationalities. Most people on these two levels quickly learned to "suck upward and kick downward" without the least hesitation. Thanks to the fact that Herman was so useful to our "capo," the inmate put in charge of the rest of us by the camp administration, we both received certain privileges.

Each barrack had a *Blockältester* (barrack captain). Under him were three or four *Stubendienst* (barrack assistants), whose duties included helping maintain order during the distribution of food. Most of the barrack captains and assistants would strike us with their clubs at the least provocation, especially when there were SS officers around.

After we had been in the barrack for an hour, they ordered us back out and told us to line up at arm-length intervals so an SS sergeant could inspect us. He addressed us briefly: "You have come to a German concentration camp, and you will work here as long as your strength permits. After that there's only one way out, and that's through the chimney." With a smug expression on his face, he pointed toward the smoking chimney of the crematorium. Since he was standing directly in front of me, I could read the words on his belt: *Gott mit uns* (God is with us). The first thought that crossed my mind was that there was no way God could be with those bastards.

As I stood there, I had a horrible feeling in my chest. I was in physical pain and having difficulty breathing, I was fully convinced that this spot where the Hungarian fascists had brought us would be our death. It seemed especially unfair that we would be executed without anyone ever finding out about it. What had we done to deserve such a cruel death in this foreign country? I desperately hoped that at least one of us would escape and tell the world—at least the people who weren't entirely indifferent—what had happened.

Sneaking into a Different Group

The sergeant inspected us one by one. When my turn came, he gave me the sign to step to the side and join the group that was to be split off from the others. Herman was to remain with the first group. Though I had no way of knowing that my group was marked for the gas chamber, I was depressed and frightened that I would be separated from my only remaining brother. I decided right then and there not to obey the order, regardless of the consequences.

When we were children, our favorite game was hide-and-seek. Since I grew up during the rough times of the 1930s, my father had to work hard just to scrape up money for food and rent, and I can't remember ever having any toys. But I was always good at hide-and-seek, and that saved my life.

As soon as I was sure that the SS sergeant and the barrack assistants no longer had their eyes on me, I started to slip away from the rest of the group, inch by inch. Quick as a wink, I slunk around the corner of the barrack and along the wall into a building that had been fixed up as a latrine. I huddled in a corner of the latrine until it began to get dark, then made my way into my brother's barrack without anyone noticing me. Some inmates from our hometown told me where Herman's cot was. We were overjoyed to see each other again.

Later in the evening, we ate our first meal at the camp. After ordering us to line up, barrack assistants led us to the barrack captain's room, where we each received a quarter loaf of bread. As soon as we returned to our cots, we heard a terrible brawl in the barrack captain's room. The reason for the commotion was that there had been no bread left when they got to the last inmate. They had realized that there must be an inmate in the barrack who didn't belong there.

The search for the impostor began immediately. I was scared to death as I watched the barrack assistants go from cot to cot with their flashlights. Pressing up against the wall, I tried to make myself as tiny as possible. Since I was far younger than anyone else in our group, it would have been easy to identify me as the culprit. But after searching for a long time, they gave up, most likely because the barrack captain didn't dare report it to the SS. No doubt he was afraid that he would be fired from his post or disciplined for failure to maintain order in his barrack.

A New Identity

At noon the next day, the authorities ordered us to go to the other end of C Camp. After we had stood in line for a while, they gave us each a tin mug, tin plate, spoon, and a ladle of soup from a 200-liter cauldron. It tasted so awful that I gave my serving to another inmate. Herman couldn't get it down, either.

Later in the day they led us to the administrative barrack and tattooed us on our left forearms with a pointed tool dipped in ink. I had a new identity. From now on I was A-8979. Herman was A-8980. An SS man gave a short speech, shrieking more than talking. We were concentration camp inmates, he told us. They would permit us to live as long as we could hold out. There was only one way out, and that was through the chimney. He finished up by saying, "*Ein Laus ist dein Todt*" (One louse will be your death).

Not Able to Help

Afterwards they lined us up along the main street of the camp to await new orders. Suddenly a huge group of teenaged boys came by, among them a friend of mine from Kolozsvar. I shouted his name, and when our eyes met, I asked him if he had seen Alexander, my younger brother. "Yes, he's here someplace," he said, "but I don't know where—there are 3,000 of us, you know."

The boys slowly vanished from sight in the direction of the gas chamber and crematorium. Smoke billowed continuously out of the chimney, and it reeked of burning flesh.

I had no chance of helping my little brother. Even if he had been able to break away from his group, he wouldn't have escaped his fate. Only by being tattooed like us could he have eluded death, at least for the time being. Nevertheless, the sight of those innocent children being herded to their death, as well as my powerlessness to save my little brother, has haunted me for more than sixty years.

Working in a Death Camp

Leon Cohen, interviewed by Gideon Greif

Leon Cohen was born in Salonika, Greece, in 1910. He was a young man of thirty when the Germans first occupied Greece. He was able to avoid capture for a time, but eventually was imprisoned and taken to Auschwitz. There, he volunteered himself and about one hundred and fifty other young Greek men for what he thought would be special work assignment doing loading at a train station. Instead, the men became Sonderkommandos. *The word literally translates as "special unit," and was used to describe the Jews who were forced to participate in the killing of other Jews.*

In this interview with Gideon Greif, Cohen describes how he had no choice but to suppress his feelings and become like a robot in order to survive in this horrible position.

[Gideon Greif:] *How were you selected for the Sonderkommando?*

[Leon Cohen:] We were taken to Birkenau that very day. In Auschwitz, the main camp, there was a small crematorium. In fact, the extermination camp in the fullest sense of the term was Birkenau. There they led us to a barracks; I don't remember its number. They quarantined us there. Afterwards, we had the numbers tattooed onto our arms.

Would you allow me to glance at the number on your arm?

Sure, go right ahead. Look—one hundred eighty-two thousand four hundred ninety-two. That was my number in Birkenau. It was my "new name." In the quarantine block, five men slept on one bunk. A few days later, some friends warned

Leon Cohen, interviewed by Gideon Greif, We Wept Without Tears: Testimonies of the Jewish Sonderkommando from Auschwitz. New Haven, CT: Yale University Press, 2005. Copyright © 2005 by Yale University and The Sue and Leonard Miller Center for Contemporary Judaic Studies at the University of Miami. All rights reserved. Reproduced by permission.

us not to join the Sonderkommando. They said that if we were forced to work there, we'd be murdered after a few months. Whoever went to the Sonderkommando had almost no chance of surviving. The Germans had no interest in preserving the lives of the eyewitnesses to their crimes.

Who warned you about the Sonderkommando?

Jews who worked near the crematoria and saw what was going on. One of them was a Jewish doctor.

Did they explain what the term "Sonderkommando" meant?

Yes, of course, in minute detail. They told us that whoever was assigned to the Sonderkommando would never get out of there alive.

We spent a month in the quarantine barracks. One day, a German visited the barracks with a Jewish doctor who was to "examine" the prisoners. Since I was fluent in German, my comrades chose me to be the interpreter. I walked over to the doctors and asked them not to take us for the Sonderkommando.

A few days later a young German, a French speaker about thirty years old, came over. He spoke with the *Blockälteste* [block leader]. The next day he approached me and asked, "You speak French, don't you?" I told him that I did and asked him what he wanted from me. Then he told me that he needed two hundred strong men to do loading work at the train station. I told them that the Greek Jews in the barracks, about two hundred men in all, could do the work. They were fit for any kind of hard work.

Obviously I believed him; I really did think he was referring to ordinary physical labor. I thought that if we demonstrated to the Germans our strength and our ability to get things done, they'd treat us well. How naïve we were back then! The man said he'd be back the next day and left. We had to get ready to march out. When I returned to my Greek friends and told them about what the young German had demanded, they asked me what kind of work we'd have to do. I calmed them and told them that we'd stay together and that we'd be fed.

The man returned the next day and said, "All the Greeks—follow me!" There were about 150 of us. It was exactly a month after we'd been quarantined. When we left the barracks, the German asked, "You know how to sing? Why aren't you singing something?" So we burst into song. There were always songs that we loved to sing together—Greek folk songs, patriotic songs, or other songs. We were still in a positive frame of mind.

Tricked into Becoming Sonderkommandos

He led us through the camp until we came to Block 13. The Germans opened the door to the barracks and ordered us to go in. We all went in. Inside, there were already some other prisoners. They asked us, "Why have you come here?" We told them that we'd come to help them with their work at the train station. One of them responded, "You idiots! This is the Sonderkommando. What train are you dreaming about?" I was so shocked and afraid that I froze on the spot. The prisoner said, "They tricked you. Believe me, this is the Sonderkommando." So they'd deceived us into joining the Sonderkommando. Later on, the prisoner turned out to be our *Blockälteste*, George.

Did you men protest when you heard about this? Did you try to reverse this grisly decree?

Protest? To whom? After we reached the barracks, the Germans locked the door on us and that was that.

From then on, then, you were part of the Sonderkommando.

Yes, that's how it happened. They divided the 150 Greeks among the four crematoria and the Sonderkommando chapter in our lives began.

When did you begin to work?

That very night. When we reached our "workplace," the Germans divided us into groups, five men in each group. When someone in my group saw what the work consisted of—cremating dead Jews—he threw himself into the flames. He couldn't bear the thought of having to cremate the bodies of his Jewish brethren.

Beginning the Work

Can you reconstruct the beginning of your work with the Sonderkommando?

On the first night in the barracks, the veteran crematorium prisoners told us about the work we'd have to do. But those stories paled in comparison to the reality.

We were stunned but few of us considered suicide. That was too easy a solution. The next morning, we walked to the camp. The Germans didn't take us to the cremation facilities but rather to the cremation pits. I saw several wagons next to the pits, and nearby was a building with a small gate. Later on, I found out that people were being gassed to death there. I waited outside for about half an hour and then we were ordered to open the doors.

The bodies fell out in one great mass and we began to load them onto the wagons. They were small open wagons, the kind that you find in coal mines, much smaller than railroad cars. We took the corpses to the pits. A layer of women's and children's corpses was placed in the pits, and on top of them was a layer of wood. Then a layer of men's corpses was put in, and so on, until the pit—which was at least three meters deep—was filled. Then the Germans poured gasoline into the pit. A bright flame rose from the mixture of bodies and wood.

What did you feel when you saw so many bodies, perhaps for the first time in your life?

What can I tell you? It was terrifying. I can't describe it in words. Just terrible.

So you worked at the cremation pits at first.

That's right.

And later on?

Later on they assigned me to work at the crematoria themselves. First, I was taken to Crematorium [IV].

How long did you stay there?

Three days. I had to leave after I had a run-in with the *Blockälteste*. That brought me to Crematorium [III], where I stayed until the end.

Describing the Crematorium

Can you describe the building?

Yes. It was a very long building. In the basement were the undressing hall and, behind it, the gas chamber, which looked like a shower room in every respect. To get to the undressing hall, you had to go down fifteen steps.

Can you describe the chamber?

Yes. It was very long. I think it was more than fifty meters long and six meters wide.

How many people could the chamber hold?

Lots. Hundreds of people. After they undressed, they were taken straight to the gas chamber.

Were the Sonderkommando men in the undressing hall all the time?

Yes. One group of Sonderkommando prisoners waited for the victims in the undressing hall. Their job was to calm the people down when they showed signs of agitation, which they did now and then. The whole process was supposed to take place quietly, without excitement and riots. The Germans couldn't tolerate that.

How many Sonderkommando prisoners were in the undressing hall?

About fifteen.

No Way to Warn Others

Did you warn the Jews that they were in a trap and that in a few moments they'd be gassed to death in the room next door?

Are you out of your mind?! To tell people such a thing? How could I tell people that they were about to be murdered? It was impossible to tell anyone this terrible truth. You have to realize that the system was too sophisticated for us to interfere in any way. The people were doomed to die and we couldn't do a thing about it. The Germans lied in the cruelest ways. We had no choice but to do as we were told. What else could we do? What could we have changed even if we had warned the people? No one had a chance of survival, neither heads of families nor their family members. No one survived. Escape was impossible. I repeat—impossible.

Was there no point in the process leading up to the murder that you could warn the victims? Couldn't you have told them that they were walking to their death?

Absolutely not. We were never left alone, even for a moment. The Germans circulated there all the time. They were the ones who'd ordered us to mislead the victims. Anyone who'd dared to tell the Jews the truth would have been murdered straight away. That is exactly what the Germans were afraid of: that chaos would erupt, a riot would break out, and the quiet process would be disrupted.

Just the same, did the Sonderkommando prisoners ever speak briefly with the victims?

Yes. In the short time they had left, people asked various questions, such as, "Where will we be sent after the disinfection? What plans do the Germans have for us?"—simple questions from people who have no idea what's going to happen to them a few minutes later.

Were they always the same questions?

Always: "Where will they take us afterwards?" "What's next?" Questions that anyone would ask. We answered that they'd be disinfected and then they'd get their clothes and

The Holocaust

possessions back and be put to work. We gave answers like those and others. I think we had no choice but to answer that way, because the idea was to dispel their fear of the unknown.

Do you think the victims believed the Sonderkommando prisoners?

I think most of them believed us. At least, that was my impression.

Do you remember a case where somebody doubted the answers or noticed something amiss?

No. Few of them imagined that they were about to die in such a cruel and imminent way. The young people were wary, but generally speaking, the people believed what they were told—at least outwardly....

The Gas Chamber

What can you tell me about the gas chamber?

I saw the gas chamber quite often. I entered it personally—after the gassing was over, of course. It was an especially repugnant job.

What did the gas chamber look like?

Like a shower room. The showerheads looked real, the whole scene was very realistic. Everyone who went in was convinced that they were about to take a shower and that the whole thing was for disinfection.

How many people could be pushed into the gas chamber?

At Crematorium [II]—as many as two thousand....

What happened after the men joined the women and the children in the gas chamber?

We noticed some disquiet.

Why?

The reason, I think, was that the people sensed that something was wrong. Maybe they'd asked the Germans and noticed that no water was coming out of the showerheads. Once I heard someone complain in this manner to the German who stood there. The German answered with fake innocence, "Really? No water? I'll take it up with Fritz. Please wait!" A few minutes later, additional Germans came, locked the door, and it was all over.

Was the process always carried out in the same order?

The women and children always came first, followed by the men. Sometimes long lines formed, since the transports brought thousands of Jews and clogged up all the crematoria.

What happened after all the people were crammed into the gas chamber?

The SS men with their canisters of gas came. They opened the windows in the ceiling of the room and poured in the gas, which looked like blue-green pebbles. This was always done, without exception, by the Germans and not by the Sonderkommando prisoners.

I remember that Sonderkommando men were called over on one occasion to open up the windows, which were covered with heavy concrete lids. Tubes led down from the openings into the gas chamber, and I took the opportunity to get a close look at the canisters of gas. The Germans who threw the gas in wore gas masks and took them off only after the lid had been closed.

After the gassing process began, did you hear voices or sounds from the gas chamber?

Of course. We heard loud screaming. Everyone screamed in the gas chamber, since they were totally desperate. Now they realized that death was approaching, so they shouted for help. I can hear the screaming to this day. It will hound me for the rest of my life. It will never go away.

Becoming a Robot

What did you feel as you heard the people screaming as they suffocated?

I've got to tell you something that's terrible but true: we'd become robots by then. We couldn't expose ourselves to the intensity of the emotions that we experienced in the course of the work. Really, a human being cannot endure the emotions that were part and parcel of our work. Once we'd repressed the emotions and felt like "normal people," we could treat everything that happened as "work" that we had to do in accordance with the Germans' orders. That's how it was. We didn't think about the horrifying aspect of our work and didn't allow any emotions to intrude. We didn't have any emotions whatsoever. We stifled them before they could emerge. . . .

[There] was a very simple elevator: a slab of sorts, open on all sides, a metal surface on which they loaded the corpses. It was an electric elevator. The bodies were placed on the loading surface and then the elevator went up.

How many bodies were loaded each time?

Fifteen to twenty. As soon as the loading began, I went up to the ground floor. That was my regular workplace.

Could you get to the ground floor from inside the building?

No, I used the stairs on the outside.

Removing the Gold Teeth

How long did you work in each shift?

Twelve hours—from six A.M. to six P.M. or six P.M. to six A.M.

What did you have to do?

Before they threw the bodies into the furnaces, I had to examine the mouths of the people who'd been murdered and rip out their gold teeth. The Germans made one of the prisoners do this work so they wouldn't lose the gold.

Were you equipped with appropriate tools for the job?

Yes. I had two different pairs of pliers to pull out the teeth, not ordinary pliers but real dentist's pliers.

The kind that are used in dental clinics?

Yes. I must say that it was a terrible, ghastly job. The bodies gave off an unbearable stench.

Didn't they have a sarcastic name for your job?

They called me and the others who did similar jobs *Dentisten* [dental technicians].

Who called you that?

The *Blockälteste*, I think.

It was a derisive name, wasn't it?

Yes, of course. The Germans also called me the "Greek dentist."

Where did you do your work?

On the ground floor, about three meters from the furnaces.

The Furnaces

What happened after you finished the job?

A signal to throw the corpses into the furnace was given. I had to signal the people to throw the corpses in. The key word was "*Einschieben!*" ["Push in!"] Every action had its own name. The people in charge of stuffing corpses into the furnaces did their work skillfully. They picked up the corpses, placed them on a little stretcher, and pushed them through the furnace door that way.

Did you also give the "Einschieben" order?

Yes. Sometimes I gave the order; sometimes the Germans gave it. It was given automatically every half-hour.

Why every half-hour?

Because that's how long it took to cremate the corpses. During that time, more corpses were taken to the ground floor and I had to continue pulling their teeth.

So you had only half an hour to pull out the gold teeth.

No, less. Only ten minutes.

How many corpses are you talking about?

Let's see. I have to count ... Sixty to seventy-five corpses in ten minutes.

How could you pull out teeth from so many bodies so quickly?

It's definitely possible. You pry the body's mouth open, look in, and if there aren't any gold teeth you go onto the next body, and so on. Sometimes it went very fast....

Coping with Horror

The first time you had to do this, you must have thought that you wouldn't be able to bear it.

Bear it or not, I had to do the work. It was repulsive but I did it. You've got to realize that there was no way to evade it. When I was at Birkenau, sometimes there was a break between one transport and the next. During that time, we had to clean the furnaces. Once the Germans found two gold teeth in the ashes while the cleaning was going on. Do you know what they did to me? They flogged me ten times on the ass, using a strap that had pieces of metal embedded in it. They accused me of sabotage and said that I'd better not to do it again.

After you pulled the gold teeth, how long was it until the other Sonderkommando prisoners took the bodies to the furnaces?

Whenever I finished one row of bodies, the German gave the "*Einschieben*" order. That was the signal to put the bodies into the furnaces.

Who trained you for your work?

I acquired my experience on the job. Believe me, I was nervous and very tense at first. I thought I wouldn't be able to do the job right and that the Germans wouldn't forgive me if I made a mistake. In other words, I thought they'd kill me if I overlooked as much as a single gold tooth. But eventually I got so good at it that I could tell which body in which row had gold teeth, a bridge, or what have you. Over time, I became an expert....

Every day you saw Jews going into the gas chamber and not coming out again. How did you put up with the work?

Ghettos and Concentration Camps

What would you do if you were in my shoes? Look, I didn't have a choice. I couldn't behave differently. During that time we had no emotions. We were totally drained. We blocked up our hearts; we were dehumanized. We worked like machines. We were human beings devoid of human emotion. We were really animals, not people. It's frightening but that's how it was—a tragedy.

Being in contact with so many dead people could drive the most stable individual out of his mind. How did you maintain your sanity?

Well, as I already told you, none of us went insane in Auschwitz since we'd stopped being people. We'd become robots.

SOCIAL ISSUES FIRSTHAND

CHAPTER 2

Life Outside the Camps

Working as a Spy

Marthe Cohn, with Wendy Holden

Marthe Cohn grew up in a Jewish family in Alsace-Lorraine, an area of France very near the German border. She was in her late teens when Adolf Hitler rose to power. When her sister was arrested and the rest of her family fled to the south of France, Cohn joined the French army. She spoke perfect German and appeared to be German because of her blond hair. These characteristics made her the perfect candidate to become a spy.

Cohn adopted the name Martha Ulrich, pretending to be a German nurse who was travelling through the German countryside looking for her fiancé, Hans, a German soldier who had disappeared. Using this as her cover story, she could convincingly hold conversations with German troops and learn about their plans, which she then relayed to commanders in the Allied forces. In this excerpt from her book, Behind Enemy Lines, *Cohn describes one such incident where she obtained information from the Germans and then risked her life to pass along the information to soldiers at a Swiss outpost.*

I must have ridden for hundreds of miles across southern Germany, garnering information and spreading propaganda wherever I could. In my role as [a German nurse named] Martha Ulrich, I became accomplished in the art of subterfuge. It felt so normal to me by then—lying to everyone I met about who I was and where I'd come from—I didn't feel at all guilty, not one little bit. It was as if I had two different personalities, and when I slipped into that of Martha Ulrich, I was so convincing, I almost believed my own stories.

The bicycle was a godsend, although it was very hard to push up mountains sometimes. Fortunately for me, there were

---

Marthe Cohn, with Wendy Holden, *Behind Enemy Lines: The True Story of a French Jewish Spy in Nazi Germany*. New York: Harmony Books, 2002. Copyright © by Beyond Entertainment, Inc. Used by permission of Harmony Books, a division of Random House, Inc. and AMG/Renaissance.

always plenty of young German soldiers around, eager to push it for me. We'd walk companionably together as I made up my elaborate stories of the French military strength and tell them how terribly afraid I was of the dark-skinned soldiers. Scores of young men would gather around, their mouths open with horror at the graphic descriptions I gave them of what was happening in Freiburg.

Mostly, these young men were in complete chaos. Many of their officers and best soldiers had either been taken prisoner by the Allies or been summoned to Berlin to form a ring of steel around it to protect it from the expected assault. The remnants of both the Nineteenth German Army and the Eighteenth SS Armee Korps were concentrated in a compact block in the southern part of the Black Forest. Their intention was to break through our front to reach either the Bavarian or Austrian Alps, or find refuge in Switzerland. For those left behind, there was little cohesion or structure. They'd been ordered to stay and defend Germany until their dying breath, but the majority seemed to be fleeing south in the hope that Switzerland would accept them. None of them had vehicles or fuel, and most had walked for miles to get there.

Meeting a German Convoy

Cycling down a steep descent on the southern edge of the Black Forest, I came across a vast convoy of German ambulances parked on one side of the road. I was surprised to come across so many vehicles with fuel in such a well-organized group. Repeating my sad story of having escaped and of my elusive search for [my fictional fiancé] Hans, I told of my sorrow at seeing the German army defeated and having lost the will to fight for our Fatherland.

One of the senior medical officers in charge of the ambulances took pity on me. "Where are you heading, *fräulein*?" he asked.

Life Outside the Camps

"To seek refuge with a family down in the plain," I replied sadly. "They were the best friends of my dear departed father and mother, killed in bombardments of Metz by the monstrous Americans."

"You poor child," he said with a sigh. "The war's been very hard on you, but don't worry, it's not over yet."

I was dying to ask what he was doing there but knew better than to question him directly. So I continued to tell of my fruitless quest for Hans and regale him with horrific tales of the scenes in Freiburg.

Learning About an Ambush

Finally, unable to keep his secret from me any longer, he looked around conspiratorially and said, "We're heading for Switzerland. The Swiss have authorized our safe transit through, from where we'll cross to Austria. But there's a little surprise awaiting the French in the Black Forest." He winked at me knowingly.

"Ah!" I said, grinning at him and nodding my compliance. "A little surprise. I like surprises."

"It's not so little, actually," he added, delighted with my giggling response. "A bloody great big one!"

"Ah, a big surprise! How marvelous!" I cried. "Do tell me more." Privately, I feared that he might be referring to Hitler's much vaunted *wunder waffen* ["wonder weapons"], and I wondered how quickly I could alert the authorities.

The colonel beamed at me, happy for the distraction of a young female audience. "An entire armored division supported by a great deal of infantry," he whispered triumphantly, "waiting in a massive ambush in the Black Forest." Unsolicited, he then told me the exact location. I thought back to the huge military camp I'd seen a few days earlier and wondered if it was one and the same.

Carrying the Message

With a firm handshake in genuine gratitude, I thanked him and pedaled off as casually as I could. As far as I could estimate, I was a good ninety miles from the nearest French unit and about fifty miles from Greta's farm on the border, where I could make contact with my antenna. It was mid-afternoon and I'd have to cycle very hard to get there before nightfall the following day. Bracing myself for a long, hard ride, I headed southwest as quickly as I could without arousing suspicion.

After five hours I'd been cycling nonstop and still seemed no nearer my destination. I'd barely paused for a drink or a rest and had eaten nothing since breakfast with Major Petit and his staff. I was absolutely shattered. When I chanced upon a remote forest restaurant I knew, I had to stop. Resting my bike against the front wall, I gingerly pushed open the door. Peering cautiously inside, I wondered whether it was safe to enter, but my hunger made me risk it. There were no other diners, just the owner and his family eating at a table at the back of the room.

Escaping Detection

The husband, at least six feet three inches tall, heavyset, with a thick neck and a small mustache, stood up to greet me. As he did so I saw that he had a highly polished Nazi party pin in his lapel.

"Heil Hitler!" he said, raising his arm in salute.

"Heil Hitler," I responded, doing likewise.

"Where have you sprung from?" he asked suspiciously.

"Freiburg," I replied quickly. "I'm very hungry. Do you have any soup?"

Having grunted that he did, he turned as if to go toward the kitchen. I noticed that he had a pronounced limp, with his bad leg scraping along the ground. It was an injury that had presumably saved him from the front. Stopping at the table at

Life Outside the Camps

which his family was seated, he said to his wife in a loud whisper, "You mark my words, that young girl's mighty suspicious. She may be an escaped foreign worker who's trying to seek refuge in Switzerland. I'm going to try and find out some more about her."

His wife, a large, square-set woman with blonde hair plaited intricately around her head, stared at me fiercely the entire time her husband was in the kitchen, heating my supper. Her three plump children did likewise. Every now and again her husband's head would appear over the wooden half-doors to the kitchen and he'd watch me closely, too.

My teeth chattering with fear and my jaw aching, I mulled over the choices in my head. I could get up and run out of the restaurant, jump on my bicycle and resume cycling, with almost no hope of out-running any pursuers. Or I could sit it out and hope to fool them. Ultimately, there was no choice.

I heard his loping gait approach and braved myself for what was to follow. As he neared with my meal, I felt like a helpless spectator watching events unfold.

The soup smelled so good. Steam rose from the huge bowl of fresh vegetables and barley and a great hunk of bread sat invitingly next to it. My stomach rumbled noisily as it was set down in front of me, and I could hardly wait to start. I dipped the spoon in and sipped at the piping hot liquid, burning the tip of my tongue.

I was aware of the restaurateur standing close by, looking down at me. Ignoring him, hunched over my bowl, I carried on rhythmically stirring my soup. Without warning, he pulled up a heavy oak chair and sat down opposite me.

"Now, tell me, *fräulein*," he said, his gray eyes piercing. "Exactly who are you and what are you doing here?"

Still stirring the soup to cool it, I broke off a hunk of bread and slotted it quickly between my lips. With my mouth full, I had a good excuse not to answer immediately and to

The Holocaust

prepare myself mentally. Taking a deep breath, I swallowed the bread and began talking very fast, looking him straight in the face.

"My name is Martha Ulrich," I said. "I'm a nurse from Lorraine. I was staying with friends in Freiburg when the French army arrived. The next morning I escaped, but I'm still terribly afraid."

"Why?" the man asked, his eyes searching for mine.

"There are so many soldiers, guns, and tanks," I said, gulping down my soup hurriedly. "And you should see all the black soldiers they have, with their white teeth and thick lips; I heard that they were raping every woman in town, and me a good Aryan girl."

I'd never eaten so fast in my life and my stomach felt stretched as I wiped the last piece of bread around the bowl. Pushing the empty plate away, with a tremulous voice I told my host how my parents had been killed in an Allied bombardment of Metz.

"I have no one left apart from my fiancé, Hans, who's a soldier, and he's missing," I wailed. I reached into my pocket and pulled out Hans's picture and his well-worn letters. "Do you think I'll ever see him again?" I asked, a convincing tremor in my voice.

The faithful party member patted my arm. "Yes, of course you will, my dear," he replied with surprising gentleness. "The might of the führer and his armies is insuperable. There has been a setback, but Hitler will rise again and so will the Fatherland. Your Hans will be safe and well somewhere. You'll be reunited with him very soon, I feel sure."

The chair was pushed back and he limped off, wandering back to his wife and children. I reached for my jacket, unfolded some food coupons and money, and stood to leave as I heard him tell her, "She's perfectly all right, poor child. She's had a very rough time."

Life Outside the Camps

A few minutes later he returned to my table to inform me that there was a whole convoy of German soldiers with assorted wagons and carts heading south on a road just west of his restaurant. "I'll take you there," he offered. "I'm sure one of them will give you a ride."

True to his word, he did. He escorted me to the road, hailed an officer, and helped lift me and my bicycle onto the back of an old pig wagon.

"*Auf Wiedersehen, fräulein*," he said, waving me good-bye. "*Gut Glück*" [good luck].

Avoiding a Roadblock

It was dark when I arrived in the next town and found myself in the small square. Sitting on a bench for a moment to rest, I was suddenly filled with the urge to stay in the town. It was about ten o'clock. Hearing footsteps, I considered hiding, but was too tired to move. An old man approached out of the shadows and asked me what I was doing there.

"I've escaped from Freiburg," I said wearily. "I'm on my way to friends, but I thought I might stop here for a while."

"Very wise, my dear," he said. "There's a huge roadblock out on the other side of the town, full of military policemen with nothing better to do than stop an old man, search his papers, and make a damn nuisance of themselves. My advice to you is not to go anywhere near it."

My lips white at the thought, I asked him if he knew anywhere I could find shelter overnight. "Certainly I do," he said. Pointing to a large town house on the opposite side of the square, he said, "See that house there? In it live the kindest ladies in town. Knock on their door and ask for their help, and they'll be sure to give it."

The man was right. The two sisters, both in their thirties, were kindness itself. They invited me in and gave me a bed for the night. Their husbands were both in the army and had disappeared. They had several children between them and shared the house. My story about Hans seemed to touch a nerve.

Meeting with Contacts

The checkpoint had disappeared the next morning, and it took me most of the next day to reach the rustic little farm near Laufenburg that had become my haven. Knocking on the door, I was greeted warmly and with open arms by the family I'd grown so fond of. Greta smiled when she noticed I was still wearing the rough green skirt she'd given me.

"I have a very important report to send," I told her as she ushered me inside. "When is your husband coming next?"

"Not for two more days," Greta replied, her face crestfallen. "He was here only this morning."

I'd missed him by a few hours, and yet it was vital that I pass my information to the French authorities as quickly as I could. I remembered the Swiss intelligence chief, Colonel Reinhart, telling me what to do if I ever needed help.

"I have to go to the border crossing at first light," I told my hosts. "I'll have to hand my information over to one of the border guards."

Their faces fell in unison. They tried to dissuade me from my plan, telling me it would be extremely dangerous. The German and the Swiss posts were not far apart, and the Germans watched for agents all the time. They had orders to shoot anyone suspicious on sight.

"Nevertheless, I must go," I told them firmly, thinking of the murderous ambush awaiting my unsuspecting compatriots in the Black Forest. "Now please fetch me a pen and paper."

Seeing they could not sway me, they did as I'd asked. I sat up all night writing out all that I'd learned in Germany, including the most important news about the ambush. There was no time to write it in code. I'd have to hand it over uncoded and hope that only the right people saw it. Sealing the

Life Outside the Camps

envelope and placing it in a jacket pocket, I wrapped a scarf around my head and left the farm at dawn with Greta and her sister.

We crept out into the little lane leading from their farm and headed for the border crossing less than a mile away. There was only the eerie glow of the gray morning light as the first strains of the dawn chorus struck up all around us. As we neared the heavy barbed-wire fence that surrounded the post, we crouched behind a large conifer and listened for patrolling Germans. Hearing nothing, Greta pointed to a small hill.

"There," she whispered. "If you climb that hill on the other side of the wire, you'll reach a road, and then you'll find the Swiss customs house on your left. The one on the other side is German, so be very careful."

Shuffling forward with me, she and her sister lifted the coiled wire, so I could crawl underneath it. With her spare hand she quickly made the sign of the cross as I squeezed her hand. Lying flat on my belly, I wriggled under the wire until I'd reached the other side without snagging my clothes. Standing, I bent over slightly as I hurried forward, concentrating hard on my destination. My left hand was in my pocket, tightly clasping the unencoded letter, which would undoubtedly cost me my life if it were ever to get into the wrong hands.

The building was dimly lit as I approached, and there was no sound. It was still dark as I reached the glass door and tapped gently on it. Standing back, looking around me constantly, I waited a few moments, but to my surprise no one answered. The Swiss are so efficient and regimented that I'd expected an answer immediately. Peering through the glass, my nose pressed against it, I quickly scanned the room, which was lit by a bare bulb hanging in the middle of the ceiling. There was no one immediately evident, but its contents made me gasp and stagger back and out of the light.

A large framed photograph of Adolf Hitler glared menacingly at me from the opposite wall. On either side of it were draped the distinctive red and black Nazi flags, bearing the swastika. Three German caps lay on the table where their owners had recently thrown them. This wasn't the Swiss post at all. It was the German one. I had inadvertently stumbled upon it, my own death warrant signed and clasped in my left hand.

Delivering the Message

Retreating, I turned and fled before the sleeping Germans awoke and discovered me there. Running back toward the road, my breath making huge clouds of steam, I saw, about a quarter mile in front of me, a very tall man step out from behind a large tree and wave his arm frantically. He was clearly signaling me to come to him. My head pounding, I hurried across to him as fast as I could and virtually fell into his arms, whereupon he pulled me quickly behind the tree.

"*Maid!*" [Lass] the huge soldier cried, speaking Swiss German. "What were you thinking? I saw you crawl under the wire and head for the German post instead of ours. Were they sleeping?"

Unable to speak, I nodded.

"How lucky can you get?" he exclaimed. "What on earth made you go there?"

Catching my breath, I replied, "I was misinformed by someone who obviously can't tell her right from her left."

The Swiss guard nodded. "Now," he said, "you'd better tell me why you've risked so much to come here."

Swallowing hard, trying to compose myself, I finally answered, "I'm a Swiss agent," as Colonel Reinhart had told me to say. Retrieving the letter from my pocket, I handed it to my savior. "This has to be delivered this morning before eleven A.M. to Colonel Reinhart in Basle. It is a matter of the utmost urgency. Please see that it gets there."

He took the letter and nodded. "It will be done, I can assure you of that," he said. Something about the way he thrust it deep into his breast pocket was deeply reassuring. "Now, where do you need to get to?" he asked. "Can I fetch you an escort?" For the first time I noticed he had very blue eyes.

"I have to go back," I told him. "My work isn't yet done. Thank you for your help."

To my very great surprise, this huge bear of a man clicked his heels together and snapped his hand crisply to his forehead.

"I salute you, *fräulein*," he told me, towering a good thirteen inches over me.

With a quick flick of my right hand, I acknowledged his salute and headed back to the barbed wire.

Forging Documents to Aid Jews

Cioma Schönhaus

The son of Russian Jewish immigrants, Cioma Schönhaus was living in Berlin at the time of World War II. His whole family had been deported and sent to concentration camps by the time he was twenty years old. Schönhaus was spared at that time because his job as a skilled worker at a munitions factory made him important to the Germans. Recognizing his artistic skills, a coworker named Walter Heyman put Schönhaus in touch with an underground network that helped Jews avoid capture. He used his skills to supply false identity papers to Jews living illegally in Germany. This excerpt from his book, The Forger, *relates the story of his first forgery.*

It was raining. After the night shift, Walter Heyman was waiting for me out on the street, under his big umbrella. He looked short next to the *Wehrmacht* [German armed forces] soldier guarding Gustav Genschow's factory.

'Well, Schönhaus, you were asking me last time why the Jews are persecuted.' On the way to the station he held up the umbrella to cover both of us. 'I told you it was because we worship an unseen God. That makes us strong—but also weak and vulnerable. An abstract God is superior to all idols. It's significant that abstract art is banned under every dictatorship. Those in power don't know what lies behind it. What's more, if you believe an unseen God is taking care of you, you feel invincible. There's a good reason why it says on every German soldier's belt buckle "God with us". But there's also a dangerous side to this Jewish conviction of being the only

Cioma Schönhaus, *The Forger*. Cambridge, MA: Da Capo Press, 2007. Copyright © 2004 by Cioma Schönhaus. Translation copyright 2007 Alan Bance. Reprinted by permission of Da Capo Press a member of Perseus Books, L.L.C.

people to have the unseen God behind them as an ally. Millennia ago the Jews developed a false view of the real world. And when they felt strong enough with their God behind them to wage war on Rome, the world power, they were defeated. And that's why we've been banished ever since antiquity. And in times like these we fight for our survival.'

Prompted by the word 'survival', Heyman went on: 'You were at applied art college. You started your training as a graphic designer. I know a woman who puts everything into saving Jews from deportation. This woman is looking for a graphic artist to help her forge a pass. Do you think you could do it? Would you like to contact her?' I agreed, and he explained: 'The woman is Edith Wolff. She is the daughter of a former editor of the *Berlin Tageblatt* newspaper. He was my boss. Her address is 79 Kaiserallee.'

Getting Started

Next morning, after the night shift, I went to see her. Her mother gave me a cool reception. Her father shut the door of his office as I entered the house. Obviously, neither of them was enthusiastic about their daughter's activities. But Edith Wolff, known to everyone as Ewo, greeted me with a radiant smile. She was small and insignificant-looking, and wore nickel-rimmed glasses. Her eyes had something chameleon-like about them. They looked in two different directions. Her hair looked as though she had cut it herself. But when she started talking, she came across as the kind of person who knows their own mind exactly. We went into the kitchen, where her friend was waiting for me. He introduced himself as Heinz (Jizchak) Schwersenz. His glance was penetrating, and his speech was rather hurried. But Ewo was in control of the situation.

It was a matter of substituting the photograph on a *Wehrmacht* discharge certificate and restoring the stamp that ran across the photo. In other words, the challenge was to imitate the official state eagle with its twelve large and twenty-four small feathers, and everything that went with it, in the right colour, with the right shape, in such a way that the stamp would stand up to any official scrutiny.

'Do you think you could do that?' 'I'll try. I've never tried it, but I reckon I can manage.' 'And what do you want for it?' 'Nothing. Well, maybe just one thing ... Herr Heyman told me you have a room where people can hide if necessary. I don't need it yet, but I might soon. I would be grateful for the address of the room.' 'Hmm, so Heyman passed that on to you.... Yes, it's a small maid's room at our cleaning lady's place. She's called Frau Lange and lives at 29 Taunusstrasse. Yes, the room is in great demand. But if you need it, I'll make sure you get it.'

How to Forge a Stamp

I was fired up by Ewo's commission. I could finally offer some resistance. At last I didn't have to just look on helplessly at what they were doing to us. I got down to work that same evening, at my desk at home. It was the desk from whose drawer the Gestapo man had taken my father's wedding ring and slipped it into his waistcoat pocket. So this was the task in hand: to change over the photograph on a *Wehrmacht* discharge certificate and forge a replacement stamp across the new photo.

Using a magnifying glass, a fine Japanese brush and watercolour paint, I copied the eagle and swastika from the stamp on the original pass owner's photograph, in exactly the original shade of purple. Then I took a sheet of newspaper, licked a blank piece to make it damp, and pressed it down on my watercolour copy of the stamp. The damp paper absorbed the paint, creating a mirror image of the stamp. All I had to do then was press the damp newspaper with the negative of the stamp on to the correct corner of Schwersenz's photo. Next, I fixed the new photograph in place with the old eyelets: the pass was complete.

I could hardly wait to deliver the forged pass. Ewo was quite taken by surprise. She had never imagined that the new photo and its stamp would look so flawless. From now on, with this pass, Schwersenz was no longer a Jew. 'You can have the room at Frau Lange's whenever you want. And there's another thing: Dr Franz Kaufmann in Halensee is looking for a graphic artist, too. I'll give you the address. Go and introduce yourself. There's a lot to do.

Assisting with Deportations

Raymond-Raoul Lambert

The Germans invaded France in 1940, and some of France became occupied territory, controlled by Germany. The rest of France was the "free zone," controlled by the French Vichy government, which at that time was enforcing many anti-Jewish policies. Raymond-Raoul Lambert was a prominent leader in the French Jewish community, and he became the general director of the Union Générale des Israélites de France. This organization had been imposed by the Vichy government to replace all other Jewish organizations.

As a community leader, Lambert was allowed to be present as Jews were loaded onto trains and deported. He gave provisions for the journey and attempted to negotiate for humane treatment for his fellow Jews. He was allowed to send children away before their parents were deported and was able to win at least temporary freedom for a few. In the end, Lambert himself was deported, and he died in a gas chamber a few days later. The following selection is an excerpt from Lambert's diary.

Sunday, August 9, [1942,] I go back up to the Milles Camp [deportation center] with [Raphael] Spanien [of the Hebrew Sheltering and Immigrant Aid Society]. My team records the "last will and testament" of peope who are to be deported. In the courtyard of the oil filling station, which has been turned into an embarkation camp, anxieties are rising. The eyes of those about to depart question me in their anguish—am I going to save them? I stiffen to ward off the emotion. I take the files to the Prefecture. Children aged two

Raymond-Raoul Lambert, *Diary of a Witness: 1940–1943*. Chicago: Ivan R. Dee, 2007. Copyright © 1985 by Librairie Arthème Fayard. English-language translation copyright © 2007 by Ivan R. Dee, Inc. All rights reserved. Courtesy of Ivan R. Dee, Publisher.

Life Outside the Camps

to fifteen will be saved. Is this humane? Their parents will entrust them to us so that they may escape this hell. During the afternoon, in the office, we prepare the equipment to be placed in the railroad cars—makeshift equipment, as if for a life raft: metal bowls, bottles, drinking cups, pails ... here in the desperate and barren peace of the Provençal countryside, a few steps away from the burnt forest, in the tile factory with its clock and its windows with holes painstakingly stuffed, in front of the little Milles railroad station, guarded by armed police. We must identify ourselves to them in order to step across the level crossing. All such deportations are organized far away from the cities, so that the criminal event will not attract notice.

Monday, August 10 is a terrible day, a heartrending spectacle. Buses are taking away seventy children from parents who are to depart that evening. I have arranged for the children to leave first so they will not see their parents subjected to the roll call.... But what a scene, under a blazing sun! We have to hold the fathers and mothers back as the buses leave the courtyard. What wailing and tears, what gestures as each poor father, faced with the moment of deportation, caresses the face of a son or daughter as if to imprint it on his fingertips! Mothers are screaming in despair, and the rest of us cannot hold back our own tears....

Then the deportees' roll call begins in the courtyard under the cruel sun. Many are felled by sunstroke, and stretchers are brought out.... The disorder intensifies the cruelty of the measures being taken.... Sitting on their suitcases, women weep and men simply wait, stupefied. All these unfortunate people have such dignity; I am astonished not to see more of them rebel, more gestures of despair. I am told later that they were given chloral hydrate in their coffee—the [calming] "mickey" before being sent into battle. Some of the policemen do not hide their distaste at having to perform such a mission. In the crowd, all sorts of reactions mingle. Some of the women have preserved a remarkably refined bearing. Some men remain impassive. Others plead with me, as if I could do anything.... I have seen and lived through two wars, but the two cataclysms have not left me with memories less worthy of humanity than these days spent in the courtyard at Milles.

The Deportees Board the Trains

The departure takes place the next morning at dawn. We can see the camp station with the railroad cars, black like hearses, waiting on the siding. The meager rations are distributed in the courtyard, where the deportees are already grouped by carloads. They are surrounded by brutal policemen who do not speak their language. They have to carry by themselves everything they are entitled to take with them. At the gate, on leaving the camp, there is a final roll call [for each carload] before they go to the station; surrounded by armed guards, forty human beings who have committed no crime are being delivered up because they are Jews, by my country which had promised them asylum, and handed over to those who will be their executioners. There are children, old people, war veterans, women, disabled people, old men.... I cannot watch each group leave the camp, I hide where I can weep.... I see people I know pass by: a lawyer from Vienna, the father of a soldier who was killed in the war, a Polish woman schoolteacher, a doctor from Antwerp, an artist who has a commission in Basel, a family with a visa for the United States.... What has become of the time when the French authorities were grateful to our agencies for helping them show the world that France was a land of asylum? I am ashamed of our powerlessness. I still hope against all hope.... Two of the refugees have just cut their wrists to escape their tragic fate. They have been bandaged and will be sent off nevertheless. Others have had nervous breakdowns and are being put aboard on stretchers. We lose count of those who fall and must be carried.

Rescue for a Few

I have spent the night in the camp and managed to obtain grace for a few from the police inspector: certain war veterans, old people, political refugees.... But I have the feeling that their fate has only been deferred.

Tuesday, August 11, the first train leaves at dawn. My team and the rabbi witness its departure. It was infinitely sad and full of dignity. There has been a suicide in the camp.

Wednesday, August 12, I go back up to Milles to try for more rescues. The condemned people are now glad to see me coming. They know that through my intervention some people were spared even after they were already on the train. This time I plead with more energy, because the scene in the courtyard has become even more tragic. Acts of despair have become more frequent, and the police reaction is so brutal that I must intervene, along with a Protestant pastor who is here. At my request, the police chief reminds his stewards that these are deportees, not detainees. To think that none of these unfortunates has committed any crime except to be born non-Aryan.

A Christian Tries to Help

Paul Zenon Wos, as told to Richard C. Lukas

Paul Zenon Wos was a member of a Christian family living in Poland during World War II. His father was a manufacturer of knitting goods and often had business dealings with Jews. When these Jews were forced into the Warsaw ghetto, Wos and his father got special passes to enter the ghetto to carry out their business. In their visits to the ghetto, they saw how poorly the Jews were treated. They befriended several Jewish families and were able to help some of them escape. Wos was a member of the Home Army, an underground military group fighting against German control. During the Warsaw uprising in 1943, Wos and his whole family were captured by the Germans and taken to Flossenburg concentration camp in Bavaria. They remained there until the end of the war.

Since pre-war times, my family had commercial dealings with Polish Jews. My father manufactured knitting goods and needed spare parts, including various types of needles. His Jewish suppliers ended up in the Warsaw Ghetto, which separated Jews and Poles during the German occupation.

Since my father and I had obtained with great difficulty special passes to enter the Ghetto to maintain commercial contacts with our Jewish wholesalers, we witnessed the horrible conditions in which the Jewish people lived. I saw with my own eyes hundreds of naked bodies lying in the streets and thousands of beggars, including many children. I can still picture, even after all these years, two Jewish girls, twins who were five or six years old, who sang and begged for food. Every time I saw them, I stopped and gave them money, even though the Germans forbade gentiles to help Jews.

Paul Zenon Wos, as told to Richard C. Lukas, *Forgotten Survivors: Polish Christians Remember the Nazi Occupation*. Lawrence: University Press of Kansas, 2004. Copyright © 2004 by the University Press of Kansas. All rights reserved. Reproduced by permission.

Life Outside the Camps

Anyone who entered or left the Ghetto had to show a pass to the police at the entrance. The papers were usually checked by the German gendarme. To my surprise, the Jewish policemen, who were also posted at the entrance to the Ghetto, often treated their fellow Jews brutally. They shouted at them and used physical force on them. I saw them beat people with their police sticks. I was sorry for the tormented people but I could not do anything about it.

Arrested by the Germans

The passes entitled my father and me to enter the Ghetto on a daily basis. I usually used the entrance at Nalewki Street because it was close to 39 Dluga Street, where our shop was located. When we met with our Jewish producers and suppliers, we usually brought small amounts of food. We had to be careful about what we took into the Ghetto because German gendarmes randomly searched us.

The first time the Germans arrested me occurred after a Jewish girl brought some needles to our factory outside of the Ghetto. Of course, she was arrested, too. Four men, dressed in civilian clothes, came to our home and searched it. They probably thought Jews were hidden there. All they found were eight twenty-dollar American gold pieces. They took the gold and intended to take me. But my mother begged them to release me. She said that they had mothers, and implored them to let me be free for her sake. One of the men sent the other three policemen outside and told my mother, "I have a mother, too and I will do it." He took the gold pieces and allowed me to go free.

The second time the German police arrested me, they sent me to the Polish police station. Ninety percent of the Polish police were involved in some way with the Polish Underground. I was supposed to be sent to Germany to work at hard labor. But after some discussion and dealing, they agreed, for 4,000 zlotys, to send someone else in my place. My father paid for the exchange.

71

The Holocaust

Helping the Jews

My daily contacts with Polish Jews in the Ghetto resulted in a friendly relationship with several families, including the Malameds, Birnbaums, Epsteins, and Landaus. The Malamed family consisted of the mother, father, a five-year-old daughter, and two sons, who were eight and ten years old. My family was involved in smuggling the Malameds out of the Ghetto before the Ghetto Uprising on April 19, 1943. We took them by horse and carriage to the former Swedish Embassy on Bagatela Street. This was a dangerous transfer because the empty building was in the middle of the German quarter in Warsaw.

To assure a safe transfer, several people were involved. My job was to stand-guard outside the building and gesture the group to enter when the coast was clear. Unfortunately, only four members of the Malamed family decided to leave the Ghetto. The grandmother refused to allow the small girl to go to the gentile side. My father tried to convince Grandmother Birnbaum, mother of Mrs. Malamed, that he would personally take care of the girl and raise her like his own daughter. Mrs. Birnbaum responded that she had already paid for a place in a bunker where she and the girl would survive the uprising. So she went to the bunker instead of leaving the Ghetto. After a few days, the Germans sent several Jews with megaphones to convince the occupants of bunkers to come out and surrender, assuring them that everyone would be safe. One of the occupants couldn't hold out any longer and he shouted he wanted to get out. The Germans located the bunker and all the occupants. They shot everyone, including Mrs. Birnbaum and the girl.

The Malameds survived the war, even though they, too, were tricked into believing there was a possibility they would be exchanged for German prisoners of war in France if they paid $100 in twenty dollar gold pieces. The Germans took their money and sent them to Bergen-Belsen concentration camp. After the war, the Malameds settled in Jerusalem and

Life Outside the Camps

Tel Aviv. I searched for them in the British zone of occupation in Germany but I missed them by two weeks. By then, they were in Israel.

We also smuggled the Landau family out of the Warsaw Ghetto, taking them to the ruins of the former Hungarian Embassy, located on the corner of Aleje Ujazdowskie and Chopin Street. There the Landaus lived in the basement with Mr. Epstein. The caretaker of the embassy supplied the family with food, medicine, and other necessities.

We lost contact with the Landaus because the Germans surrounded the area with barbed wire after the assassination of SS General Franz Kutschera, "the Butcher of Warsaw," whose headquarters were located not far from the Hungarian Embassy. After that, the Warsaw Uprising broke out and we had no further contact with the Landau family and Mr. Epstein because we lived in a different area of the city during the uprising. After the Poles surrendered, the Germans took us to concentration camps. After the war, I learned from the caretaker that the Landaus, in the hands of the Germans, had left the ruined city after the Warsaw Uprising. I don't know whether they survived the war. Mr. Epstein died in the basement of the building and was buried there.

My sister, Irena, had agreed to find a home for the six-year-old son of Mr. and Mrs. Neufeld. The boy was placed in the home of a friend, Zygmunt Cieslikowski, who lived on Sapierzynska Street near the Ghetto. A few days before the Warsaw Uprising, the Germans found out that the boy was with Mr. Cieslikowski. They searched the apartment and took the boy and Mr. Cieslikowski to the backyard where they shot them. The parents of the boy died in one of the German death camps. The parents of Mr. Cieslikowski refused to talk with Irena because they blamed her for the death of their son.

The Warsaw Uprising

When the Warsaw Uprising began in August 1944, my family lived in the Old Town section of the city. The Germans di-

The Holocaust

vided the city into sectors which they systematically destroyed, killing Home Army soldiers and civilians. After thirty days of fighting, Old Town had to capitulate. I was a member of a Home Army unit that was to deploy through the sewer system to Srodmiescie, the central section of the city. But the sewer through which we were supposed to evacuate was blocked by German mines and burning gasoline.

I decided to join my family on Miodowa Street. It took two hours to get there; in normal times, it was a fifteen-minute walk. I no sooner rejoined my family when suddenly we heard loud shouting, "*Polnische Banditen!*" All Polish resistance fighters were called "bandits" by the Germans.

The Germans marched us out of Warsaw to Pruszkow. On our way out of Warsaw, one of the Ukrainian soldiers who was part of a unit under German command tried to steal my mother's gold wedding band off her finger. My mother shouted to a German officer, who reprimanded the soldier and sent him away from the column of Poles.

It took several hours to reach Pruszkow by foot. After we arrived, the Germans separated the old people from the younger ones. My mother, refusing to be separated from her family, pleaded with the SS officer to allow her to remain with her children. The SS man said, "You must be a crazy Pole," but allowed her to stay with the rest of the family.

They ordered us into cattle cars, which took us on a two-week journey to Flossenburg [a concentration camp in Bavaria]. We were tired, dirty, and hungry but still together—my parents, two sisters, my aunt Zofia, a cousin, our cook, and me.

At the Concentration Camp

It took us a few hours to get from the depot to the concentration camp. We were met by an SS physician. The other medical personnel were fellow prisoners. One of the members of the medical team was Janusz Janicki, a Pole, who warned us

Life Outside the Camps

not to give away all of our belongings because the Germans would confiscate them. He suggested that we give them to him and he would return them after the obligatory bath. I did what Janicki suggested. Other people in our group lost all of their belongings. Janicki proved to be an honest and most helpful man, who helped us to survive the camp.

The Germans segregated us. They sent doctors to clean latrines and engineers to dig trenches, standing in knee-high water. A great number of them did not survive the hard work. We had to endure endless roll calls and stood for hours when someone managed to escape.

When an escapee was caught, the Germans hanged him in front of all of the inmates in the camp. Almost every other day, the Germans executed Poles, mostly members of the Polish Underground who had been arrested in Lublin and sent to Flossenburg.

Extremely dangerous work in the stone quarry and at the nearby repair shop for damaged German fighter aircraft caused many people to die. There was terrible hunger in the camp. My father, claiming his soup didn't taste good, gave me his portion. I was recuperating from typhus and my father knew I needed extra nourishment. I remember one day when the SS searched for a German shepherd that belonged to one of them. The dog was never found. The prisoners had eaten him.

People who had died and had gold teeth became the prey of the Germans. It was routine procedure for the gold teeth to be pulled out, after which the corpse was marked with red paint as "clean" and ready for cremation in the camp crematorium.

The crematorium operated around the clock and could not keep up with the number of corpses. The procession of prisoners carrying two corpses on one stretcher left daily through the main gate on their way to the crematorium outside the camp. At the main gate, there was a coke burner with iron rods inside. The SS men checked whether the people

The Holocaust

were actually dead by placing a hot iron rod to their stomachs. In keeping with German efficiency, they kept meticulous records of every prisoner, dead or alive.

Shortly before the Allied liberation, the camp was flooded with prisoners evacuated from other concentration camps located in the east. Many evacuees to Flossenburg came from Auschwitz.

The Germans Evacuate the Camp

Finally, the Germans decided to evacuate Flossenburg. Large groups, each consisting of thousands of prisoners, were marched out of the camp under SS escort. The only inmates left were those in the hospital, including the medical personnel. Prisoners unable to walk were placed up against the wall of the camp's bath, where the SS men shot them with pistols. The notorious "Bloody Alois" from Auschwitz participated in these shootings.

The blood and brains of the executed people covered the eight-foot-wall. After the execution of those who were unable to walk, the Germans ordered us in the hospital to carry the corpses to the roll call area, where the bodies were stacked in layers between wooden logs. The number of corpses were several hundred or perhaps several thousand; I lost count. Then the Germans ordered us to burn the bodies. The odor of burning bodies was indescribable, causing us to vomit.

After the Germans ordered the remaining prisoners to march out, we were left in the camp hospital without guards. But we knew that the SS men would return to liquidate the hospital as well as the patients. Prisoners in the hospital prepared to fight the SS men when they returned. The night passed quietly. But the SS men did not return.

Saved by the Americans

The next day we heard rifle shots. In a few hours, we saw the first group of American soldiers. An outburst of indescribable

Life Outside the Camps

joy exploded. Prisoners were so overcome they kissed the boots of the American soldiers. They cried and knelt before them. It was difficult for us to comprehend that the Americans, not the hated SS, were there among us.

The liberation of the camp by the United States Army saved my life and the lives of other prisoners in the camp. If the American soldiers had arrived later, probably all of us who remained in Flossenburg would have been executed by the SS.

Belonging to the Hitler Youth Organization

Hubert Lutz, interviewed by Eric A. Johnson and Karl-Heinz Reuband

Hubert Lutz was only four years old, living with his family in the German city of Cologne, when Adolf Hitler was appointed chancellor of Germany in 1933. When his father, who was unemployed, attended a meeting of the Nazi Party, he was impressed by what he heard and decided to join. The Nazis helped him get a job, which improved the family's financial situation.

In this interview with Eric A. Johnson, Lutz recalls his experiences as a member of the Hitler Youth. He attended his first Hitler Youth meeting at the age of seven. Many of his older friends were already members. Lutz remained a member for ten years. He was not interested in the politics of the organization, but he found it exciting to be a member, especially during bombing raids when the group would rescue people and help them find shelter. Lutz reports that at the time, he and his friends were vaguely aware that Jews were being killed. They believed the Jews were killed as punishment for anti-Nazi activities or died of starvation in the camps. It wasn't until after the war that he learned of the mass exterminations of Jews and others in gas chambers.

In January 1933, when the Nazis took over, I was not yet five years old. I remember very clearly all the writings on the sidewalks with swastikas and the hammer and sickle and people yelling and marching and all that. Then came a big commotion and people said that the Nazis won. A short while after that, when my father ... was at the unemployment of-

Hubert Lutz, interviewed by Eric A. Johnson and Karl-Heinz Reuband, *What We Knew: Terror, Mass Murder, and Everyday Life in Nazi Germany: An Oral History.* Cambridge, MA: Basic Books, 2005. Copyright © 2005 by Eric A. Johnson and Karl-Heinz Reuband. Reprinted by permission of Basic Books a member of Perseus Books, L.L.C.

fice, he ran into his company commander from WWI. It was sort of a big surprise. This company commander then invited my father to come to a meeting of some party. I don't know whether he was an official or officer or whatever, but it turned out to be the Nazi Party. So he went to one of the gatherings, was very impressed, and came back as a member of the Nazi Party wearing a brown uniform. Up to this day I don't know where the money came from. We sure didn't have any money to buy that, so there must have been somebody who furnished uniforms for people.

That would have been in 1933, and from then on my father was gone most of the time working for the Nazi Party. My father was born in 1900, so he was thirty-three years old at the time. What exactly he did, I don't know. He was not paid; he was still on unemployment. But then his new party friends found him a job. I don't know the exact date when this happened. This was when the unions were closed down. The Nazis established what they considered a replacement for the former socialist unions. Dad did office work, clerical work, and that was when he got paid. It was not a high-paying job, and there was a problem, by the way, in that the Nazis demanded that any man who was working should not permit his wife to work also. My mother was not supposed to have a job; they had to keep that a little bit quiet. On the money that he was making at the NSBO [National Socialist Shop Cell Organization], we just couldn't live.

Because of their slightly improved income, my parents moved into a modern housing project in the suburb of Zollstock, where, at the age of seven, I joined the Hitler Youth. I remember this very distinctly. We used to play on the street, all the kids. Then one day my friends said, "We have to go to a meeting." I asked about the meeting and they said, "Why don't you come along? Why don't you come and join us?" They were all members of the Hitler Youth, which up to that time I hadn't even realized.

The Holocaust

Joining the Hitler Youth

[Eric A. Johnson:] *So this was when you joined the Hitler Youth. What was it like?*

[Hubert Lutz:] Yes, it was the *Jungvolk* [young people], the *Pimpfen* [youngest subsection of Hitler Youth]. So I went with them and I remember that the guy in charge of the group, who was maybe three years older than I was, said, "What do you know about drills and such?" My father and I had played soldiers at home, so I showed him what I knew, like about-face and all these commands. He was impressed and said, "Fine, join." It was something that, to us kids, did not have any political content whatsoever. I remained a member of the Hitler Youth from seven to seventeen.

Whenever you have kids at that age, around ten years, or twelve years and younger, you have to maintain discipline. The discipline in the Hitler Youth was maintained simply by having certain punishments. For instance, if you talked out of turn, you were punished by not being allowed to wear your scarf for three weeks. That was not for really severe crimes; it was for clowning around or whatever. The other punishment was a more severe punishment. Part of our uniform was a dagger. Can you imagine a ten-year-old carrying a dagger? It was an honor to be allowed to wear that. If you did something really nasty, you were not allowed to wear your scarf and your dagger and that meant that you were like an outcast. If something worse happened, they would send you home and you had to work it out with your parents. That worked really well. . . .

Hearing About the Murder of Jews

What was the Gestapo officer [Hubert Nordstern] like who lived in your building between 1937 and 1943?

We lived on the ground floor and he lived on the floor above us. He was very friendly to me, to everybody. But there was one person in the house, and this was the guy that lived

Life Outside the Camps

on the same ground floor as we lived on, who was deathly afraid of Nordstern just because Nordstern was a Gestapo officer. The rest of the people in our house felt at ease with him.

Nordstern was, I would say, in his beginning thirties. He was younger than my father and had two boys. He talked to me rather often. One of the things I had was a tendency to walk slumped over, and he would say to me, "Walk straight, or I'll kick you in the ass." He liked me and he felt because of this he had some parental authority or so. My dad would be the same way. It was not as harsh as it may sound; it was a friendly reminder.

Did he ever relate anything to you or your family about the murder of the Jews?

Yes, that was in 1943 after a bombing raid. After the bombing raids we had received special rations. Part of the special rations for adults was coffee, real coffee, so my mother had some coffee. We were all shaken up because of the raid, and I had been out firefighting. I came back early in the morning to take a nap and I heard my mother talking to Mrs. Nordstern in the kitchen. Her husband had been visiting for a few days [on leave from the eastern front], and then had to move on. And then she said to my mother, "Mrs. Lutz, do you know where my husband is?" My mother said, "No." And she said, "Well, he is in the hospital. He had a nervous breakdown. The nervous breakdown was because they are killing people, women and children, in Poland and in Russia." And my mother said, "I can't believe that." And she said, "Yes, he told me a story where somebody shot a woman, took her baby, hit the baby, and grabbed the baby by the legs and bashed its head against a wall." My mother said, "I cannot believe this. There is nobody who would do that."

My mother was in total denial, there is no doubt about that. But it was about so-called partisan cleanup actions. They supposedly wiped out partisans, which were a big problem for the German army. The partisans were really effective at blowing up trains and so on. So the German approach was, if they knew there were partisans in the village itself, to wipe out the village. And that's what they did. It was not mentioned in the reports that those were Jewish people. Just imagine: they shot a woman and they took the baby. Somebody took the baby and killed the baby by smashing its brains out!

The reports we heard were always presented as antipartisan activities. Now that doesn't make the killing of women and children acceptable by any means. But there is a slight difference here between fighting partisans, who were actually attacking you and fighting you, and rounding up Jews and killing people who were not really doing a damn thing to you and so on. But you also have to see that Russia had refused to obey the Geneva conventions. And, in addition, the British had made it very clear that they bombed women and children to weaken the home front. So I think a lot of people thought, "Okay, if that's what you want, that's what you get."

But did you not hear specifically about the murder of Jews?

We heard about a transport of people going out. There were rumors that people were killed, but there was never any mention of gas chambers. There were rumors that said people were squeezed together in these camps and most died of typhoid fever. And that was in essence the execution style. Now, about shootings, that was in connection with the partisans. Nevertheless, I am sure that they rounded up Jewish people and executed them along with the other partisans. I didn't really give it any thought. I was fifteen, sixteen years old. We heard this on the periphery. That was not, to kids of my age at the time, our primary interest.

When Jewish people were disappearing on these transports, what did you think?

We didn't think about it. No, we didn't even think about it. They were out of sight. I'm talking about people who are fifteen years old. And there were the bombing raids and there were questions about food.

Life Outside the Camps

There weren't very many Jews, first of all. Even at the time when all the Jews were still in Cologne, you hardly ever saw any Jewish people where we lived in the Cologne suburbs of Sülz and Klettenberg. There were very few Jews who lived out there. For us kids there was no reason to talk about that, because we didn't see them disappear. So we didn't see these roundups that they talk about, where the people were put in streetcar loads and sent to the Messegelände [Cologne Congress Hall] from where the Cologne Jews were deported to the east. I never saw that. Very few people did see that. Still, there are a number of people, more than two or three or ten, that did see it. But compared to the 750,000 people who lived in Cologne, they were a small minority, that's all.

Attacks on the Jews

What about what happened on Kristallnacht? [November 7, 1938, when Jews and their property were attacked throughout Germany] *Did you see that?*

Yes, I did. There was only one Jewish store in my neighborhood. And when I went to school in the morning, I didn't even go by that toy store, because that wasn't on my route to school. Other kids came and said, "There are toys all over the place, all over the place!" But, first of all, once we came to school, our teachers told us not to go, not to look at that. And, when they could, they informed the parents that they should take their kids and keep them away from that stuff for safety reasons. Anyway, they made an effort to make sure that the kids didn't see it. I think I saw it only a couple of days later.

I did see the burned-out synagogue, the one on the Horst Wessel Platz on the Roonstrasse. That was the big synagogue for us. That was around for a long time throughout the war. Yes, I did see that. But did it impress me? No, because there were so many burned-out houses all over what used to be the Horst Wessel Platz.

The Holocaust

What do you remember about anti-Semitic propaganda?

Well, for one, there was the *Stürmer* magazine. Nobody in my family would ever touch that thing. It was, some people called it, pornographic. I mean, it was real, heavy-duty anti-Semitism, usually purchased by members of the SS. But I don't know anybody in my circle, among my friends, social democrats or Nazis or whatever, who ever read this. The *Stürmer* was displayed more publicly. They started out, by the way, placing it in glass window boxes and they ended up covering these boxes with mesh wire because the glass windows were often shattered. So that shows you there were some people who were not very happy with that. We kids used to go and look at it, became it was wild stuff. It was pornographic, not in the sense of showing nudity or girls or something, but it was real low-grade type of propaganda given to the people. I would say it was the *National Enquirer* equivalent in the Nazi Party. Truth didn't mean anything; distortion was enormous. It was almost like reading dirty fairy tales. So that was one example of propaganda. During the war there were also a number of propaganda movies.

Mostly we felt, however, that we were being propagandized in terms of the allegedly positive aspects of the Nazi program. That was pounded into us. But it was on such a theoretical level that somebody in his early teens was turned off. We didn't want to hear political education.

What did you think about Hitler? What did the people around you think about him?

He was admired, very much admired. We all really loved him. We felt that he could do no wrong. Whenever something went wrong or was obviously wrong, people tended to blame it on the underlings. I'd only seen him twice, and the length of time was for ten seconds each time. So I can't base any opinion on that. I do remember that there were lots of pictures of him, though. As a matter of fact, in our office at the *Ortsgruppe* [local] party headquarters, there was a picture of a little girl handing him a bouquet of flowers. Also we had this image of him feeding a little deer and being seen with his Blondie, his German shepherd dog. And you saw him breaking ground for the Autobahn, shoveling dirt and so on. He had the image of a savior, and he was looking for that. He was idolized to the point that when I was eight years old I asked myself, "What happens if he dies? He does everything."

What did you do when Hitler died on April 30, 1945, a day after your birthday? Were you sad?

I ate my birthday cake. No, it wasn't a sad birthday. I remember when they said the German army surrendered, my mother said, "Thank God! This stuff is over." But, for my father, the world collapsed.

In general, what was it like for you to live in the Third Reich?

To us, it was the most exciting time of our lives. As a Hitler Youth, you liked action, you liked to show what a tough guy you are. You know, like fighting fires and dragging people out from under the rubble; wearing your steel helmet and having a cigarette in the corner of your mouth. We didn't know any better. You see, when the Nazis came to power, I was five years old. I grew up in this, so it was a normal way of life to me.

So it just seemed normal to you?

Yes. Sometimes when we had Hitler Youth meetings in the early days we did these so-called military drills. I found them boring. I had done that a thousand times, and we went again and I'd find that boring. Then again I learned to circumvent certain inconveniences by, for instance, volunteering for training in the signal corps. I learned Morse code. To them it was cheap military training. When we were drafted eventually, some of us knew how to fly an airplane, some of us knew how to run radio equipment. But, to us kids, working with real military transmitters and using Morse code and

The Holocaust

being up there right with the big shots in the military made us feel good. It made us feel important.

Learning More after the War

When did you first hear that Jews were being murdered in great numbers?

In great numbers, I would say 1948, 1949. We knew about concentration camps. In 1945 after the war there were a lot of people running around and showing their numbers, their tattoo numbers. There were some pictures that were shown right at the end of the war, like when they liberated Dachau, Buchenwald. But that to us was almost understandable because the pictures they showed were of people that had obviously died from starvation. You could see their skeletons. We had not been through that kind of a starvation, but we knew how quickly you lose your weight. And there was also the word that most of these people had died from typhoid fever. And there were many other typhoid cases, for instance, in France and in Buchenwald. So, yes, that was not excusable. On the other hand, there were times at the end of the war when a lot of our people didn't have anything to eat.

What about the gassing and the shootings?

We tried not to believe it. We simply said, "No, that's too brutal, too gruesome too organized." Quite frankly, I began to read more and study more about it when I was in this country after 1959. A lot of people asked me, "How come you guys didn't know this? You claim you didn't know anything about it." And, I asked myself, "Well, how come you didn't know this?" So I started reading a lot and I started, well, maybe reading with a biased mind, hoping that I would find reason to believe that it was not true. But the evidence piled up. This became more convincing by the day. So I also asked myself, "Could we have done anything different? Where did the responsibility lie?" My conclusion was the responsibility lies in the fact that people didn't do anything about it. They just stood by and closed their eyes and ears. And I think that is true. People just didn't want to believe it. They didn't.

SOCIAL ISSUES
FIRSTHAND

CHAPTER 3

Liberation

Leaving Auschwitz

Agi Rubin and Henry Greenspan

Agi Rubin was in her mid-teens when she was deported to a concentration camp, first to Auschwitz and later to Ravensbruck. Most of her family died in the camps, although she was reunited with her father after the war. The following selection includes Rubin's diary entries from April 1945; each entry is preceded by Rubin's recollections of that period, written decades later.

After being liberated from the concentration camp, Rubin and her companions first were taken to a barn, where Allied soldiers fed and cared for them. They were then taken to a hospital where they stayed until the Russians came. Rubin talks about how difficult it was for them to believe that they were truly being liberated and not just being moved to another concentration camp. She also describes the horrified and compassionate reactions the soldiers had to what she calls the "girl-skeletons from Auschwitz."

Liberation came in steps, and the next day it stepped closer. We began to meet the soldiers who were really in charge of the camp: British, French, Belgians, Yugoslavs, and more. Apparently they had an understanding with the Germans that they would take over as the *Wehrmacht*, [German armed forces] withdrew before the Soviet advance, and this next day was the start of the transition. The barn where we had been left was adjacent to the camp itself.

The Allied soldiers had heard of the death camps, but we were the first people they had seen who had been there. And, notwithstanding all the combat they had experienced, seeing us—we girl-skeletons from Auschwitz—somehow overwhelmed them. As they led us from the barn, into the camp,

---

Agi Rubin and Henry Greenspan, *Reflections: Auschwitz, Memory, and a Life Recreated.* St. Paul, MN: Paragon House, 2006. Copyright © 2006 by Agi Rubin and Henry Greenspan. All rights reserved. Reproduced by permission.

89

The Holocaust

and on to the hospital, they formed a kind of spontaneous honor guard. By the time we reached the hospital, there were literally two rows of soldiers, one on each side of us, which was their way of welcoming us and paying respect to what they sensed we had endured. Their responsiveness was genuine, and their care and compassion were extraordinary.

As my diary makes clear, while describing our last hours in the barn and then our move to the hospital, it took a while for us to believe that we were truly safe—the the bread would be there tomorrow, that the hospital was really a hospital. Still, looking back, I am surprised that we could feel so quickly that we belonged to the world again. It was because these good men, our liberators, were the world that welcomed us.

April 21, 1945

We get up and look around the room. And soon we meet our companions in the barn. They are Hungarians, Poles, Russians, French. They do not make a very good first impression on me.

The sun comes in. Food is arriving. Bread, margarine, and black coffee—things that we haven't seen in many weeks. To us, this is a fairy tale, a Cinderella story. We could have eaten all the bread. There was enough to fill us. But we didn't dare. "What will happen tomorrow?" We look at it and put it aside.

As the healthiest among us three, I go to work. I bring water and wash the sick ones. The morning goes by quickly. Sleeping, eating, drinking coffee, washing ourselves for the first time in months. Noon comes and dinner arrives—a two-course meal! Soup and a potato. So we are kept busy. We are under shelter and getting food. But we are afraid of having to go back on the march. So we don't eat everything.

In the afternoon, we are surprised by a policeman at the window who speaks Hungarian. He had served in Germany. We spoke with him, and he promised to bring us milk in the

Liberation

evening. We are looking forward to that reunion. But he disappeared. We never saw him again.

There is dead silence in the room. Suddenly the door opens, and with the opening of this door we are brought back to our lives. A clean-cut officer enters whom I like immediately. And other officers too. An unusual sight—they are not Germans, yet they wear military uniforms. But these are our friends. They come in and bring smiles and contentment. We don't know who they are. We only know that they are good.

One bends down. But before he does, he looks like he is afraid of something. He says to us, *"Juden?"* [Jews]. Then he looks off to the side, and tries to hold back his tears. He leaves the room, wipes his eyes, and returns.

With the kindest, most compassionate words, he tries to comfort us. He tells us that he has been a prisoner-of-war, a Jew. He and his comrades are going to take us to the hospital, which he says is a good place. But suddenly we are unsure. "A hospital? What is this? A trick?" All three of us answer in horror that we are healthy. We are afraid to go to this hospital. But the Jewish friend whose name we don't yet know stops the words in our mouths. "Don't be afraid. We are taking you to a good place. A place where we will take care of you."

Soon we gather ourselves and our belongings—a quarter of a bread and a potato. The wind is biting. We walk alongside this Jewish man. The rain that hits our faces almost raises our spirits. But they are still the faces of tired, broken prisoners, completely in a daze.

As we walk, I think of those from our transport still on the march—still being harassed, kicked, herded along. Suddenly a police car approaches us and stops. It goes on its way, and we continue our journey. Eventually, we come to the hospital.

In the courtyard, new faces greet us. These men look at us with astonishment. We are still in our dirty camp clothes, so it is not surprising that they are shocked by our appearance. We go down a hallway, into one of the rooms, where we are met by Frenchmen. We don't speak each other's languages, but we understand their kindness and compassion. Soon we are able to take warm showers and then to sink into bed. How good it feels!

The room fills with inquiring Frenchmen, Yugoslavs, British, and others of many nationalities. They are soldiers, former prisoners-of-war, who had not seen anyone like us before. They are interested in our fate. And when they leave, they bid good-bye with sadness and sensitivity in their eyes. They don't want to overly disturb us.

Now a bucketful of sweet milk arrives, and everyone can have as much as they want. And we don't have to stand in line for it! This didn't happen to us in the German camps. And now this has happened too!

Next, a very kind-looking French doctor comes in. He goes around and writes down everybody's ailment on his chart. Yes, we have come to experience this too!

I am here in a prisoner-of-war camp—me, as a woman, as a child. The American and English care packages come, and they provide what we need in the camp. After dinner, the doctor says good night. He wishes us rest and peace. "By tomorrow, not one German will remain here at the hospital. They will no longer rule over us at all!" We take his word for it and sink toward sleep. For the first time since I can't remember, we can stretch out on white sheets. We can rest. They are not going to wake us in the morning for the roll call, for the *Zehlappel*.

Rebuilding a Life

After a while, it became almost routine. The men would enter our room, take a look at us, and start to cry. And we, still not really understanding how we looked or what it meant to them to see us, began to giggle. One group would walk out; another would come in. We winked at each other: "They are going to cry again." And so they did. They cried, and we laughed.

For three months they cared for us, nurturing us back to life with food and milk and kindness. But the first man, the one who had asked us if we were Jewish, stands out among them all. This was Marco, who became a lifelong friend. He was our teacher and our guide—especially in those first crucial weeks. For us, it was like being born again. He was that little corner that I could only dream about in Auschwitz. My mother was gone and could not be replaced. But the memories of care and of belonging—the feelings themselves—were a foundation that could be built upon again.

Of course, there were other memories too, and they continued to rage within me in these first days of liberation and, I would learn, in all the years to come. That is what comes through in the next day's writing—the compulsion to remember and to retell; the wish for silence and for peace. It would be many years before I would learn that this dilemma has no resolution. It is a contradiction you live, not solve.

April 22, 1945

From out of a deep sleep we wake for breakfast. Hot tea is awaiting us. From the potatoes that remain, I fix a good puree that we spread over the bread. We still restrict ourselves to one slice of bread only. We may need the rest for tomorrow. But the biggest specialty at home wouldn't have tasted as good as this English tea and pureed potato. Hungry people appreciate anything that signifies food.

After breakfast, we get a very helpful visitor who brings us men's shirts and underwear. It doesn't matter—it's clean. We are no longer scratching and always imagining the lice.

Many of the visitors' names we don't know. And there are so many. But among them is the Jewish man who brought us to this hospital. He takes the three of us as his sisters. His name is Marco Rubinovich, from Belgrade.

All the men are courteous and kind, but this one is special. His name we must write down, and even if we didn't we would remember. From his story, I learn that he went through some of the same suffering as we. He lost his family. But he himself didn't suffer as much because he was a prisoner-of-war and treated as a soldier through political arrangements. Thus he hadn't seen the Auschwitz crematoria, but only heard about them. Only through our stories did he learn what was done.

It's enough to listen to these horrors. The gas, the crematoria, the forced marches. It's enough to hear about it, let alone to have to see it. So that is enough of this for now.

Marco comes in very often and always arrives with news. "Be happy. Tomorrow, or the day after at the latest, we will be completely free. All the German dogs have left the hospital already. We are done with them. Brothers, sisters, rejoice!"

The poor man was wasting his breath trying to make us feel good. We still don't believe anything.

Up until the last moment, the crematorium is our nightmare. We are telling everybody about it, whether we want to or not. Our stories are only about the crematorium, whether we want to or not. Either in my dream or when I am awake, I only see the flames in front of me. And the vision never fades.

Too much talk tires us, so it's better for us to rest. The visitors are courteous. They would like to stay longer, but the doctor makes them leave.

So this is our new life. The day goes fast, and it is good. But now it is quiet. It's night. Let's sleep. Let's dream we shall be happy.

The Russians Arrive

The next day was the official liberation day—the arrival of the Russians. For us it was also the beginning of new questions: Where was home? What was home? What would we find there? And whom?

In some ways, this little hospital in no man's land had already become a home. We felt like comrades, and so we were. Some of the soldiers wanted to take us with them, and every time a group of them was transported home, after the liberation itself, they invited us along. "You come with us. You'll be a part of our family." They meant it. A Frenchman said, "I have two daughters. We will have five daughters. I am a poor man. But we'll make do. Come, you will be our family."

There were enticements. But, in the end, there was really no question. We had to go home first, home to Munkacs [Hungary], to see.

April 23, 1945—The Liberation Day

There is a lot of commotion in the hallway. We wake up wondering—maybe it's our liberators? We don't wait very long because the men rush in with great joy. "The Russians are here! Rejoice! We are free! In a week or two, Germany will be completely kaput!"

Later on, a very high-ranking Russian officer and his retinue come in. Our friend Marco is with them as their interpreter. His face glows with happiness. He introduces us to the officer. We show him the number on our arms that we received in Auschwitz. The officer shakes his head. "This is unusual. There are very few."

This is not the way I pictured the liberation. It's not true. I don't believe it. "They can still take us back," I think to myself with fear. But I don't say anything out loud. The high-ranking officer kindly says good-bye.

In the room we just look at each other. We can't speak. Everybody's eyes are filled with tears. But nobody dares to show it.

What now? Everybody can go wherever they want when they are healthy. Now we are free. We are no longer under the Germans.

The Holocaust

Later, Marco comes back and asks if we want to go to Palestine. He can register the three of us as Palestinian or as British citizens. He tells us that Munkacs will be under the Russians. And once that happens, we will not be able to leave.

We ask for some time to think about it. After a few hours, we decide to stay with our initial feeling: we are going home. We are going home to look around our town. And after that we will emigrate somewhere. Marco agrees with our plan, although he fears it might then be too late to get out. But he doesn't want to argue with us. In a case like this, you can't tell someone what to do. So we will be registered as Munkacsi and as Hungarians.

We talk about the past and the future. And about the future and the past. We have suffered enough. Now good will come. Let the sunshine brighten our life.

As far as food is concerned, it's not even news anymore. I think we could get back very fast to a regular life—a normal, human way of life, as we were used to years before.

I was liberated in a prisoner-of-war camp among very fine people. They took care of us with goodwill and compassion. Life is unusual. And so is this liberation. Who knows where my poor father is suffering? Who knows what he is thinking about his family among whom hardly anyone remains? Who knows where he is liberated? Who knows where and when I will see him again?

Father, you are alone, and you are my only thought. I am liberated, but I am afraid to go home. I am afraid what I will find, what I will not find. But let's wait now. We shall see what will happen. Let there be peace. Peace of mind.

Freedom Arrives at Oberaltstadt

Helen Freeman, as told to Joseph Freeman

Helen Freeman was born Chaja Borenkraut (nicknamed Chaiale) in 1921 in Radom, a city near Warsaw, Poland. She grew up in a large, comfortable Jewish family. Aside from Freeman, only one brother and an aunt survived the Holocaust. After the war she married Joseph Freeman, a man she had met in the camps, and took on the first name of Helen.

Freeman's husband, Joseph, has written several books about his own experiences during the Holocaust and recorded his wife's story in Kingdom of Night, *from which this excerpt was taken. When her family was deported, Freeman was young and able-bodied. After four months in Auschwitz, she was transferred to Oberaltstadt labor camp, a subcamp of Gross Rosen concentration camp in Poland. At the time of the liberation she was exhausted, hungry, and at the point of despair. When she was set free, she could think of nothing but returning to her home to look for her family. Discovering they were not there took away all sense of hope, until someone directed her to where an aunt was living. From there, she began to build a new life.*

On the night of May 7, [1945,] I could not sleep at all. The hunger and the noises in my stomach made me feel dizzy and weak. I couldn't take any more. It was too much for me. Penetrating the darkness of the night was the thunder from the heavy guns and the streaks of light cutting across the horizon, one after the other. The ground shook from falling bombs. We sat in the dark room for hours, waiting and waiting, as the noises grew louder and louder, the bombs seemingly falling closer to where we were.

Helen Freeman, as told to Joseph Freeman, *Kingdom of Night: The Saga of a Woman's Struggle for Survival.* Lanham, MD: University Press of America, Inc., 2006. Copyright © 2006 by University Press of America, Inc. All rights reserved. Reproduced by permission.

The Holocaust

As the dawn broke we heard voices in Yiddish calling loudly, "*Die SS zenen verschwinden*" ("The SS [an elite Nazi military force] have disappeared"). Still afraid, we did not move. Then came loud voices and a knocking on the door. A voice rang out, proclaiming: "We are free. No more Germans around." Still afraid, I could not believe it. A few minutes passed before I realized what had happened. It was a shock to me. Slowly, I moved my weary body to the window and looked down. I saw many of my friends running around, jumping. I opened the window and could hear laughter—the voices of so-called slaves, singing and dancing. Turning around, looking at my sick friends, I stared to cry, but this time I shed tears of joy. I felt overwhelmed and confused. What do I do now? What will become of us?

I collected myself and went outside to where they had buried Henia Stern. I stood there and thought how sad it was that she didn't live to enjoy this moment. Already in some places grass was growing around the few stones marking her grave. Shaking my head and patting the ground, I raised my eyes to the sky, pleading: "Lord, didn't we suffer enough. Please take care of her young soul. I am lost with nowhere to go. Please guide me. I don't know what to do."

I was a survivor—alive, but sick in body and soul. This was the moment I had hoped for, free from physical pain and no longer afraid. Yet I wasn't truly free. Where to go? What will I do? I am alone. I found it very difficult to accept the changes that had just taken place.

The Americans Arrive

At first Russian soldiers entered our camp, but they were soon replaced by American GIs. Now we no longer had to scavenge for food. The American soldiers provided us with plenty to eat and I voraciously devoured anything I could get my hands on. I ate without end, but my system couldn't take it and I became sick, as was the case with so many others. Once the

Americans realized that we could not handle unlimited quantities of food, they set up special kitchens that carefully doled out portions we could digest. Our liberators provided medical help for the sick as well, but many former prisoners died. Some perished because they were too sick; others got diarrhea from overeating. Some expired because they could not take the changes; it just became too much for them. Many of them were single survivors, the only members of their families to escape liquidation at the hands of the Nazis. Alone, feeble, and nowhere to go, they lost their will to live and soon after liberation died in their sick beds. It was so sad. So many died. There was so much suffering and starvation—living skeletons just waiting to die, despite their newfound freedom.

The Americans took good care of us, providing us with clothes and shoes. Most importantly for us women, we could wash. Slowly we started to look human again. But despite the welcome changes, we had difficulty adjusting to our new conditions. I spent sleepless nights wondering if and when I would see my family. How about my mother and father? How about my brothers? Did they survive? I cried and prayed to the Almighty for their safety. I clung to the hope that some of my family managed to survive the Nazi scourge. Maybe mother. Or maybe my father had survived. They had been in the bloom of their lives. I couldn't think about my brothers. The last time I had seen them was on the way to Tomaszow [ghetto]. Just thinking of losing them made me feel terribly alone. Sometimes I would dream of [my brother] Fishel. Oh, I loved him with all my heart.

At the age of twenty-three all I had were memories of my home and my family. I couldn't forget the last words Fishel had spoken to me in 1943 at the liquidation of the small ghetto in Radom [Poland]: "Chaiale, I have vowed to our father that I will do everything possible to take care of you. I remember our father's last words. 'Don't forget Chaiale. This is my only daughter. Take care of her.'" Whenever I could I would turn to the Almighty and ask Him to take care of Fishel. Only after that would I ask the Almighty to take care of me and give me the strength and the energy to face my painful destiny.

Searching for Family

Now, at the moment when I was free, I could only think of getting to Radom to see Fishel. I was debilitated and in pain, but the hope of seeing my family gave me the will to overcome my sickness. I asked [another woman named] Henia if she would accompany me to Radom. She answered: "I will go with you. I, too, am looking for your brother Sam. I am alone. Maybe he survived. He is the only one for whom I have to look. My family, all of them, were sent to [the death camp] Treblinka in 1942 at the liquidation of the ghetto. Yes, I will go with you."

At the end of May 1945, Europe was in chaos. Roads were engorged with refugees from every country, some trying to leave, some returning and some wandering aimlessly. We Holocaust survivors presented unique problems which the occupation authorities were not prepared to deal with. They set up temporary facilities for survivors called displaced persons camps, or DP camps. Many survivors stayed in the camps while trying to decide where to go for permanent residence. Some left the camps, and with no other place to go, wandered from one country to another. Others tried to return to their places of birth, looking for members of their families who perhaps had withstood the Nazi slaughter. Survivors found it difficult to believe that the Nazis had murdered most of their kin, but the hope of reconnecting with loved ones kept them going.

When I was liberated, the Americans told us to go back to our hometowns. For some of us, home was Germany, the land of the exterminators. And many Germans still continued to regard survivors as racial inferiors who threatened their blood

Liberation

and their soil. Others took to the road to return to Poland, home to three million Jews before the war.

At the end of May 1945, the guns were silenced. Since there were no frontiers, it made it easy to move from one country to another, especially in those parts occupied by the victors. The occupying forces tried to help the survivors to get to their places of origin, but transportation presented a huge problem in Eastern Europe where railroads had been destroyed. Consequently, roads in all directions swarmed with refugees traveling on foot, by horse and by military vehicle.

I was liberated in northern Czechoslovakia, not on German soil, so I felt safe traveling about. The Czechs, having suffered tremendously at the hands of the Nazis, were very friendly to survivors, offering food and shelter. The route to Poland went through Prague, where international groups and American Jewish organizations fed and housed us. In this capital of the Czech Republic I met many Jewish people, survivors from Poland.

It took several days to get the appropriate papers before Henia and I were on our way to Radom. Again, I was filled with anxiety about my family, wondering whether any were still alive. I was afraid not knowing whom I would meet coming back to my house in Radom. I found comfort in thinking about my relatives. I hoped to see them. It had been so many years since I had seen my mother. What about my father? How about Fishel and my other brothers? It was torture for me, just thinking that some of them might have perished. I prayed to God to give me strength so that I could face the moment of meeting them.

The last hours before arriving at Radom were for me the most nerve-wracking; my heart beat so loudly. I was sweating. I felt so excited I could not wait. The moment the train pulled into Radom, I grabbed Henia by the hand and ran from the station toward the house where I grew up. I could not believe what I saw along the way: The streets had not changed; they were just as I remembered. I walked along Trauguta Street, then on to Zeromskiego Street. I could see houses from both sides of the street. All were the same as when I had left the city.

Disappointment

Tears rolled down my face as I approached the corner of Walowa Street, not far from my home. It looked to me just as it had always been. Coming to the corner of Walowa and Peretza, I had to stop and take a deep breath. I was only a few houses away from my home. Excited, I yelled, "Henia, just a few more houses and I will be back with my family." I still believed that I would see all of them. Coming to my house at Peretza 3, I did not look, just ran up the steps. I knocked at the door, breathlessly waiting to see which one of my loved ones would open it. Someone inside responded; the noise of the turning key opening the door made me feel nervous. Shaking with anticipation, I got ready to greet someone from my family. What happened then I never will forget. A strange man opened the door, looked at me and scornfully uttered, "*Co ty szukasz Zyd?*" ("What are you looking for, Jew?"). Choking with tears, trembling, I could barely speak. Finally, I said, "My, my family used to live here." He slammed the door in front of me, hollering, "Never come back. The Germans killed your family. This is not your home anymore."

For seconds I was frozen at the entrance to the building. I was in shock; in an instant my dreams were completely shattered. This was the most devastating moment in my life. Still, I couldn't believe it. I looked at the door again and again to make sure I was in the right place. Yes, it was the apartment where my family and I had lived. Everything was the same. But this familiar place was suddenly now strange and hostile.

I couldn't take any more. I ran down the steps, crying. I couldn't talk. Henia embraced me. The only words that came out from both of us were, "What will we do?" We had to cry to let out our disappointment and bitterness. Where were we to go? Strangers passed us on the street, animated in conversation. Then, surprisingly, we heard some people speaking in Yiddish. Approaching them, we found out that some Jews were now living in the city. We went with them to the Pasternaks, people who had known my family. At last we had a place to stay. But I was still depressed and confused, feeling very much alone.

The desire to see my family had kept me alive; now, I didn't have any desire to go on. Everything was gone. I was a lost soul in a country that had become the graveyard of my family, my people. That night I could only sleep a few minutes—awakening, shaking. I couldn't make peace with my sad reality. The Pasternaks had been one of the few families to survive the carnage. Two brothers, a sister, a sister-in-law, Sonia Zlotnik, along with her brother and her two sisters emerged from the Holocaust to start a new life. I was so envious. There was not a single surviving member of my family, just me.

Through the window the moon was on the horizon, spreading its dull light. The blinking stars made me forget my grief for but a second. Sorrow, humiliation, and personal tragedy had followed me in my youth. I didn't have time to grow up. I had been exposed to a life of cruel and painful struggle at such a tender age. Now I was free once again, but I felt more grief than when I was in the hands of the murderers. At least in the camps I had hope that some day I would be reunited with my loved ones. Now, this too, was taken from me. Even in the barracks I could dream and think of better tomorrows; now, I didn't have one.

New Hope

It was a long and painful night. In the morning Shewa Pasternak came into my room and said: "Chaiale, I know how hard it is for you. But remember, Sonia Zlotnik once was at Szkolna camp. There she told us that your aunt Frania Fink, your father's sister, was in Warszawa, where she stood as a beggar in front of a church. Why don't you go to where she lived in Zamosc? Do not give up. Maybe she is there." I looked at her, "Yes, I remember. You were there at the same barracks when Sonia came in and told you about her. But I forgot. Too many things have been on my mind. Now you have given me some hope."

While we [were] there, other Jews came to the Pasternak's house. They, too, had been wandering from city to city looking for surviving members of their families. Shewa asked them where they came from. They recounted that two days ago, as they were passing through Zamosc, they stayed at the home of Frania Fink, the only Jew in town. Shewa shouted, "Chaiale, didn't I tell you to go there? Never lose hope. You aren't alone any more. Your Aunt Frania is alive; go there."

Finding Family

Turning to Henia I said, "You, too, are coming with me. Wherever I go, you, too, are going." She didn't say a word, just nodded her head. Shewa packed a bundle with food for us and soon we were on the road to Zamosc. After traveling a few days by truck, by horse and by carriage, we reached the city. It took no time at all to find my aunt, since she was well known in Zamosc.

My aunt sat with me for hours sharing her anguish and painful life during the war. During the occupation my aunt had sold her hardware store to a Polish friend, with the understanding that in case some of the family survived he would sell it back to them after the war, which he did.

For more than thirty years our family had lived in this little town where gentiles lived in peace with their Jewish neighbors. Their children grew up together, played together, and attended the same schools. The only difference was their religion. Friday afternoons the Jews closed their enterprises in

Liberation

preparation for the Sabbath. The Christian Polish population observed Sundays for their religious practices. Sometimes there were little disturbances, but mostly the population continued to live and to conduct its business without any uneasiness.

That was the relationship before the Nazis occupied this area of Poland. Everything changed after September 1939, when the Nazis built a wall between the Polish and Jewish population. As I was listening I could not believe how this woman had overcome the hardships she had endured during the past six years. The story of her survival was no less incredible than mine.

The Trials at Nuremberg

Richard W. Sonnenfeldt

In December 1944, Richard W. Sonnenfeldt was a twenty-two-year-old private in the American army. He had been born in Germany and spoke both German and English fluently. After being called upon by General William "Wild Bill" Donovan, head of the Office of Strategic Services, to interpret an interview with a witness in preparation for the war crimes trials, Sonnenfeldt was immediately put on a plane to Paris to begin work as an interpreter.

Sonnenfeldt advanced quickly as an interpreter and became the chief interpreter at the war crimes trials in Nuremberg. He served as interpreter for the top Nazi officers on trial. In this excerpt from his book, Witness to Nuremberg, Sonnenfeldt describes the interviews with Reichsmarschall Hermann Göring, Hitler's second in command.

Shortly after my arrival at Nuremberg, Herman Göring was to be interrogated by Colonel [John] Amen [chief interrogator for the American prosecutor]. Before his suicide, [Adolf] Hitler had named Göring his official successor. He had been described as a jolly and venal fat man with the instincts of a barracuda, the heft of an elephant, and the greed and cunning of a jackal. He was a man with brains and no conscience. So, as Amen's interpreter, I was to meet Göring, who had the imposing title of Reichsmarschall, a "six-star" rank created especially and only for him. Göring was more familiarly known as *Der Dicke* (Fatso).

When Göring surrendered to the American army, he acted as though he was celebrity, like Napoleon on his way to Elba. He had brought with him a large staff and a dozen suitcases.

Richard W. Sonnenfeldt, *Witness to Nuremberg*. New York: Arcade Publishing, 2006. Copyright © 2002, 2006 by Richard W. Sonnenfeldt. All rights reserved. Courtesy of Arcade Publishing.

Liberation

Prior to being lodged in the jail in Nuremberg, he had been held in two locations where he had charmed or intimidated interpreters. I had transcripts of his interrogations by Military Intelligence in Mondorf, where he had been very arrogant when confronted with questions based on newspaper reports and common knowledge of his activities. He had confused his questioners, who did not have the captured documents we were now studying, with haughty, irrelevant replies. Now Göring, in Nuremberg as a material witness and a likely defendant, was incarcerated in the maximum security, starkly uncomfortable Nuremberg jail.

By now I knew from captured documents that Göring was a decorated flying ace of World War I. He had succeeded Manfred von Richthofen, the famed Red Baron, as squadron commander. His father had been governor of Germany's colony Southwest Africa. His mother had made the long trip to Germany so that he could be born there, and left him in the charge of a nurse. As an adult, he had good connections with the old imperial officers and also with right-wing industrialists. Between the world wars, he had been the first commander of the SA (the Nazi militia) and the organizer of the Gestapo as a national force of terror and head of the newly established Luftwaffe [the German air force]—which had been forbidden by the Treaty of Versailles. As the head of the Gestapo, he had arrested politicians who opposed the Nazis, and as president of the Reichstag he had proclaimed the Nuremberg Laws, which terminated the civil rights of German Jews. He had been the man of iron in the bloodless capture of Austria when Hitler almost lost his nerve, and he was the bomber of Rotterdam. He was also the man who had ordered my father to be put into a concentration camp and later ordered him to be released because he had earned the Iron Cross in World War I! Now Göring was the most senior surviving Nazi. His actions as the number-two Nazi indicated that he was deeply involved in Hitler's conspiratorial drive to war.

The Holocaust

Pretrial Interrogations

I wondered how he would react to me when we put him under oath for pretrial investigations. Although I had already interpreted interrogations of other once-exalted Nazis, some of them fluent in English, I felt apprehensive about the impending encounter with Göring. He had been such a legend while I was a youngster in Germany, so feared while I was a frightened refugee in England when the RAF was desperately fighting off his Luftwaffe. At Nuremberg, as I anticipated meeting Göring, I felt the Jewish refugee I had once been tugging at my sleeve.

Our interrogation room, Number One, like a half dozen others on the second floor in the Palace of Justice, was near an enclosed stairway that led to the jail. The room itself was bare, without a carpet on the polished terrazzo floor. Colonel Amen, the interrogator, sat at a plain wooden table with his back to the window. The witness would sit across from him, with the light from the window in his face. I sat at the narrow end of the table with Colonel Amen to my left, the witness chair to my right, and a stenographer slightly behind me. An armed guard would stand in the corner at the opposite end of the table.

Now with the door ajar, we heard shuffling footsteps. And there, accompanied by a white-helmeted guard, was Göring, in his faded gray uniform, with discolored rectangles on the collar and the lapels where his marshal's insignia had been. With felt boots provided by his jailer to protect his feet from the cold stone floors, he was being weaned from drugs—about forty pills a day of a derivative of morphine—and his face was puffy and gray. Breathing heavily, he was apparently exhausted from dragging himself up the stairs from his prison cell. But as he entered, I noticed that his eyes were alert, his eyebrows were slightly raised, and he moved deliberately, somehow managing to keep an aura of authority. I looked at his hands, now stripped of the huge rings he had once worn. With no jeweled field marshal's baton to clasp, his fingers were trembling, ever so slightly. He undoubtedly realized that this was going to be different from previous sessions, which had been quasi-social occasions. He knew that we were here to get him to incriminate himself and that he was here to defend himself.

Not a word of greeting was exchanged. Colonel Amen motioned him to sit down, and then the guard walked behind him to his right. For Colonel Amen, I translated: "State your name."

"Reichsmarschall Hermann Göring," he said.

"Record that as Hermann Göring," said Colonel Amen to the stenographer.

Now Colonel Amen addressed me: "State your name." I did. And then, "Hold up your right hand. Do you swear that you will accurately, completely, and truthfully translate my questions from English into German, and the answers of the witness from German into English?"

I said, "I do."

That was the first time I was formally sworn in as an interpreter. From now on, my swearing-in would be repeated for every pretrial interrogation. I resolved to be extra careful. Next the court stenographer was sworn to record accurately in English everything that was said. And so we began.

I translated, "Do you, Hermann Göring, swear that you will tell the truth, the whole truth, and nothing but the truth?"

"First, I want to know, am I before the judge?" countered Göring.

As I translated, I tried to assume alternately the voice and mien of Amen, the bloodhound New York prosecutor of Murder Incorporated, and of Göring, now a caged and clever rogue trying to confound his captors.

"I ask the questions here and you answer them," said Amen to Göring. I translated Amen's rejoinder into German, but Göring tried to correct my translation. Amen whispered to me: "Don't let him interrupt you."

The Holocaust

Teaching Göring How to Behave

Suddenly, I thought of Churchill's remark of Germans being either at your throat or at your feet. I asked Amen for permission to teach this witness how to conduct himself with me. "Go to it," said Amen.

I also remembered the captured German general whom I had forced to walk in front of the truck carrying his men after he complained that he did not want to ride to prison camp in the back of the truck with subordinates. Simultaneously I remembered an old joke about Göring. I said, "Herr Gering"—a deliberate mispronunciation of his name I had heard as a child. The word *gering* means "little nothing" in German. I said: "Herr Gering. When I translate the colonel's questions into German and your answers into English, you keep quiet until I am finished. You don't interrupt. When the stenographer has recorded my translation, you may tell me whether you have a problem, and then I will decide whether it is necessary to consider your comments. Or, if you would like to be interrogated without an interpreter, just say so, and I will merely listen and correct you."

His eyes flickered, and he gave me a long look. He said, "My name is Göring, not Gering."

He knew that it was to his advantage to have an interpreter. While his English was good enough to catch the gist of questions asked in English, it was not good enough for him to assert himself, which was what he really wanted to do. Why else would he talk to the Americans at all when he could be silent? Besides, hearing questions first in English and then in German gave him an advantage. The delay made it much more difficult for Colonel Amen to surprise him, and, since everything had to be said and repeated in two languages, we could ask only half as many questions in a given session.

I said. "I am the chief interpreter here, and if you will never again interrupt me, I will never again mispronounce your name, Herr Göring." Colonel Amen watched our facial

Liberation

expressions and waited patiently during this interchange. I turned to him and said, "Prisoner Göring will now answer your questions."

From then on Göring demanded that I be his interpreter. Göring was the Chief Defendant, Amen was the Chief Interrogator, and I was the Chief Interpreter. All in apple-pie German order! Later it became known that I was Göring's favorite interpreter, and I never knew whether to be proud of that fact or resent it. And so we began interrogating him. . . .

As I interpreted these various conversations, I understood the full extent of the ghastly crimes that had been committed against millions of innocent humans by powerful men without morals or conscience. I became a passionate believer that Göring and his cohorts had to be convicted and punished in an international legal proceeding that must not ever be mistaken by fair-minded people as mere revenge by victors or vengeful survivors over the vanquished. I also saw the Nuremberg trial as a never-to-recur opportunity to write the history of Nazi Germany by extracting it under oath from those who made it the crime of the century. . . .

Describing Göring

I learned [from various interrogations] that besides Hitler, only Göring was charismatic and powerful enough to have had a German constituency of his own. Perhaps his followers were besotted by his geniality and attracted by the jolly mirth of a fat man, convenient covers for his cunning and satanic initiatives. In the early days of Hitler's regime he was the man of action. I learned that his evil genius had made the Gestapo into a state-sanctioned instrument of terror, and that he had been inventive in bending the power of the state to his own acquisitive ends. He also had used his official power to persecute personal enemies while promoting favorites. He had laughingly perverted truth, lacing his venality with isolated good deeds to impress his humanitarian half-brother or to indulge some weird streak of sentimentality—which fooled people into thinking he knew right from wrong. Göring used to lounge about in his hunting lodge with rouge on his cheeks, huge ornate rings on his pudgy fingers, and a flowing toga enfolding his ample girth. I did wonder why his actress wife, Emmy Sonnemann, who had a daughter by him, remained vocally and demonstratively loyal to him to the end. She criticized her husband only when Hitler ordered Göring to be executed for trying to exercise his powers as designated deputy when he believed Hitler was irredeemably trapped in his Berlin bunker.

Göring was extraordinarily versatile. When he nominated Erhard Milch as commanding general of the Luftwaffe under him, jealous rivals complained that Milch had a Jewish father, a Nazi liability if ever there was one. As chief of the Gestapo, Göring arranged for proof that Milch's real father was a full-blooded Aryan who had had an extramarital relationship with Milch's gentile mother. To memorialize this feat, Göring proclaimed: "I decide who is a Jew and who is not a Jew." When I reminded him of that episode, he slapped his thigh with mirth at his own great wit. No one ever encapsulated the difference between the rule of law and the rule of man so pithily.

Göring was also versatile when it came to first courting, then emasculating the powerful German army generals of the old school who would not accept Hitler's leadership. In 1933, when Hitler become chancellor and Göring became Reich minister without portfolio, traditionalist high-ranking officers of the army maintained their loyalty to [Paul Von] Hindenburg, the revered Generalfeldmarschall of World War I and president of Germany. Looking down on Hitler, they considered him, an ex–lance corporal, a mere enlisted man, to be an ignorant, uneducated, and dangerous adventurer. Still, they recognized that Hitler's loyal SA militia, the nearly one million jackbooted storm troopers, were dangerous adversaries to their small army, which was restricted to one hundred thousand by the Treaty of Versailles.

In 1934, Hitler tried to buy the loyalty of the generals by directing the assassination of Ernst Röhm, head of his own SA. Hitler claimed that Röhm and his lieutenants were planning a seizure of power. Göring and Himmler, who then still reported to Göring, were astute enough to be Hitler's executioners in that vile plot. Göring was in charge of the assassinations in Berlin—reported to be about one thousand. The murder of Röhm and his top lieutenants appeased the army's top generals but did not buy their enthusiasm for Hitler's leadership. When I asked Göring how he felt about the murder of his friend Röhm, he responded chillingly, "He was in our way." . . .

How Göring Attempted to Seize Role as War Minister

In a spectacular series of maneuvers, Göring plotted to seize leadership of the armed forces and other uniformed services of Germany and nearly succeeded. After the murder of Röhm, well over a million SA storm troopers were put under Göring's control. As Himmler's senior, he would also effectively control the Gestapo, the police, and the SS. Göring began maneuvering to be named minister of war, head of the traditional armed forces. Two senior conservative army leaders stood in his way.

First, Göring went after top-ranking, sixty-year-old General Werner von Blomberg, minister of war. Göring had discovered that Blomberg was marrying a notorious prostitute, and made sure Hitler was invited to the wedding. Afterwards he told Hitler of his shocking "discovery" about the bride. As atonement for this embarrassment of the führer, Göring made Blomberg resign to avoid a public scandal.

Göring's next target was General Werner von Fritsch, the supreme commander of the army, the highest-ranking officer under Blomberg. Fritsch would normally have been Blomberg's successor as minister of war. The Gestapo targeted a notorious and sleazy homosexual who was made to claim he had sex with Fritsch in a Berlin railroad station lavatory. Göring had Hitler stand behind a curtain in the Reich Chancellery while this plant "confessed" the affair to a Gestapo thug. That eliminated Fritsch, despite the fact that a court of investigation headed by Göring later found the charges false.

But Hitler was not outfoxed by his lieutenant. He abolished the war ministry and named himself supreme commander of the armed forces. All soldiers, from Göring and the generals on down, had to swear fealty to Hitler personally as their supreme military commander.

Remaining loyal to his führer who had outsmarted him, Göring settled for Hitler's offer to name him Germany's highest-ranking officer; later Hitler also named Göring his official successor as head of state. With his old imperial army training, which demanded loyalty, Göring then served Hitler until defeat was certain for the führer, marooned in his Berlin bunker.

Göring Brags About How the German People Were Duped

At Nuremberg, Göring continued to display his versatility. He tried to deny complicity in planning an aggressive war, and he denied participating in or commanding war crimes, genocide, and crimes against peace. Yet he continued to brag extensively about his role, as the number-two Nazi, in subjugating Germany by demolishing democracy (not a crime being tried by the tribunal). When asked whether the German people had wanted war, he explained breezily how easy it was to dupe them:

"Why, of course, the people don't want war. Why would some poor slob on a farm want to risk his life in a war when the best he can get out of it is to come back to his farm in one piece? Naturally, the common people don't want war, neither in Russia nor in England, nor in America, nor in Germany. That is understood. But, after all, it is the leaders of the country who determine the policy and it is always a simple matter to drag the people along, whether it is a democracy or a fascist dictatorship or a parliament or a Communist dictatorship. The people can always be brought to the bidding of the leaders. That is easy. All you have to do is tell them they are being attacked and denounce the pacifists for lack of patriotism and for exposing the country to danger. It works the same way in any country."

At Nuremberg, Göring declared repeatedly, with inclusive sweeps of his once-bejeweled hands, that he would take responsibility for all that was done in his name, while at the same time he denied knowledge of virtually everything that had been done in his name. Unlike [Joachim Von] Ribbentrop [Hitler's foreign minister], he did not babble, he just repeated this one explanation: "You don't think, do you, that I could ever know all of the nonsense that went on in my many offices? I had so much to do. But if you have papers that I signed or that I saw, then I accept responsibility for what my subordinates did."

Göring did claim that he was deceived and misinformed by overzealous colleagues like Heinrich Himmler, who had committed suicide, and Martin Bormann, who had disappeared. When asked directly about some atrocity, Göring always answered, "It is possible that I heard something about that, but I had so many official roles, and I spent so much time giving the führer my advice; I was so busy and important. How can you expect me to remember such details now?"

Göring Denies Knowledge of Camps

Throughout the interrogations, Göring insisted that Hitler knew little of concentration camps and even less of exterminations, mass starvation, and all the other "regrettable" abuses that had been perpetrated in secrecy by that conveniently dead fiend Heinrich Himmler. And if Hitler did not know about extermination camps, how could Göring have known?

The Holocaust

Too bad that Himmler was dead! Describing the evil Himmler, Göring once commented to Amen, "My dear Colonel, you would have enjoyed questioning that man." As though talking about the Holocaust were some kind of fun.

As slippery as he was, occasionally I could catch him. Göring had sometimes been used by Albert, his younger half-brother, an improbable humanitarian who claimed he had befriended many that had been persecuted by the Nazis. Ensign Bill Jackson, the son of Justice [Robert H.] Jackson [chief American prosecutor], and I suspected Göring's brother of having taken money for his help in freeing concentration camp inmates. He was a diffident witness who constantly volunteered information for which we had not asked. But several, including the famous composer Franz Lehar, attested to Albert's munificent humanity, corroborating his story. At his brother's urging, Göring repeatedly arranged the release of concentration camp prisoners who should never have been imprisoned. Perhaps brother Albert thought that reporting reprieves arranged by brother Hermann would create mitigating circumstances for him, but it did not work out that way.

"You testified that you had nothing to do with putting people in prison or concentration camps," I said to Göring one day.

"Yes, I told you that many times," he replied.

"How then could you get prisoners released when you had no power to have them incarcerated?" I asked.

He grinned. "*Ach so*," he said.

Touché! I thought.

Göring told prison psychologist Dr. Gustave Gilbert that he expected to have marble monuments erected for him as a German hero thirty years hence. When I heard this, I mentioned it to him and he said, "It won't matter that my body isn't there. Napoleon's body is not in his grave either." No doubt about it, Göring had charisma, a naturally powerful bearing, and limitless ambition.

CHAPTER 4

Lasting Effects of the Holocaust

Hitler Killed My Father

Shirley Paryzer Levy

Shirley Paryzer Levy grew up in Brooklyn, New York, the daughter of Holocaust survivors. From the time she was a child, her mother told her stories about her experiences in the concentration camps during the Holocaust. Her father, on the other hand, would not speak of the camps at all until shortly before he died. At that time, he made a series of recordings of his memories for Levy. She couldn't bear to listen to the pain in his voice. In this article, Levy explains why she blames Hitler for her father's death, even though he lived for many years after the war was over.

He wouldn't talk about the years he spent in Nazi concentration camps. But they never left him.

I am approaching another anniversary of my father's death. It will be more than a dozen years since he passed away. I still don't agree with the cause of death on the certificate. The cause of death, according to the doctor, was cancer. That was not what killed my father. The cause of death was Adolf Hitler. My father was a Holocaust survivor. He lived and breathed being a Holocaust survivor. It defined him. It is on his tombstone. His whole life in America revolved around World War II. It was evident in his everyday life. I remember when we were in a hotel in the Catskill Mountains one summer, and there was a fly zapper in front of the lobby. My father heard the noise, saw the flies and mosquitoes get zapped and very quietly said, "That's how Hitler did it, too." There was no escaping his past.

I grew up in the Crown Heights section of Brooklyn, a small community filled with European Jews. The synagogue

Shirley Paryzer Levy, "Hitler Killed My Father," *Newsweek*, May 5, 2008, p. 22. Copyright © 2008 Newsweek, Inc. All rights reserved. Reproduced by permission.

where my father prayed was filled with men and women who were survivors as well. It wasn't until I was in the third grade that I made friends for the first time with children whose parents were American-born. I did not believe you could be Jewish and not suffer as much as my parents. They came to America, the "golden medina" (golden country), to enjoy the freedom of religion and the freedom of speech, and just to be free. They were not free, however, from their past and their nightmares.

I marveled at my parents' ability to live normal lives. To go through hell for four years (they were living in Poland, and the Polish Jews were the first to be shipped off to concentration camps) and still be able to go to work and make a decent living was beyond my ken. They celebrated bar mitzvahs and weddings with their friends and families, and went on vacations as if they were true Americans. I was miserable. I wanted to shout at them, "Why are you acting normal when I'm not?" I was afraid the Nazis were going to knock on our door and it would be my turn to go. Isn't that how they went off to the camps?

Holocaust Stories from One Parent, Silence from the Other

When I was growing up, my father never talked about his time in concentration camps (he was moved around to several). My mother, also a Holocaust survivor, did all the talking. I never knew who Dr. Seuss was, or even heard of Goldilocks or Rapunzel. My bedtime stories were about how my mother stole a potato and made it last for three days. My father's brother told us about how he cheated the Nazis by hiding under the bodies of prisoners they had shot and pushed into ditches. My father never said a word.

When the movie "Schindler's List" opened, my parents went to see it. I couldn't believe them. I yelled at my father, "Why did you have to see what you've already lived through?

The Holocaust

Why subject yourself to more pain?" My father answered that he had an obligation to go. He said the world had to see what it was like, and he had to go to be a part of it. He was so proud when members of the Shoah Foundation asked him to be recorded for the Holocaust Memorial Museum. He lived in Arizona at the time, and they went to his house for the interview. In front of the camera he told his story. He now lives on in the archives with other survivors.

When my father felt the end was near, he started to obsess about his past. He decided that if he didn't start talking about the Holocaust, who would remember? He made a series of audiotapes beginning with his life in Europe, leading up to the Holocaust and ending with his wedding to my mother in Germany in 1946. When he finished the tapes—there were seven in all—he mailed them to me. He would ask me at least once a week if I'd listened to them. I told him no; I just couldn't, because there was pain in his voice and I couldn't bear to hear it. A year after he died I tried to listen to the tapes. I could not. I knew he was no longer suffering, but I would not be able to tell him that I knew he was finally at peace.

I don't know if he felt the Nazis would rise again, but I know for sure Hitler never left him. A friend of mine who recently lost her mother told me that two weeks before her death, her mother started acting in a way that made my friend think she was hallucinating about being back in a concentration camp. She was once again being tormented by the Nazis. We agreed Hitler got her in the end. Just as he got my father. Hitler didn't end at 6 million. He is still killing the Jews. It is 6 million and counting.

Lessons to Be Learned from the Holocaust

Anthony Lipmann

Anthony Lipmann's parents were so secretive about being Holocaust survivors that he didn't even realize he was Jewish until he was sixteen. When he was a child, he saw the number tattooed on his mother's arm from her time at a concentration camp and assumed everyone's mother had one. Finally discovering his Jewish heritage prompted Lipmann to read and learn about the Holocaust. In this selection, Lipmann relates his family history and also his belief that Jews have a duty not to perpetuate hate so that the Holocaust does not happen again.

It is a long way from the barbed wire of Auschwitz to the crenellated towers of St James's Palace [London], but by the end of the month my mother will have made the journey. On 27 January [2005], Holocaust Memorial Day, she will join 600 concentration camp survivors to mark the 60th anniversary of liberation at a private reception at the Palace.

My mother is 80, having been born in Vienna in 1924. She survived not just Auschwitz but Theresienstadt, Bergen-Belsen and Salzwedel. She was 19 when she was transported to Theresienstadt from Vienna in November 1943, 20 when she was liberated from Salzwedel in April 1945. Her story—at any rate as much of it as she is prepared to tell—is contained in a handful of letters she wrote after liberation, one of which, written on 20 November 1945 to my aunt in London, serves as an affidavit of her time in the camps. It includes an account of her arrival at Auschwitz with her parents on 12 October 1944 after two days and one night on the transports:

> We found ourselves in a very bleak area; totally flat, either swampy or covered with huge rocks. We entered the camp

Anthony Lipmann, "How I became a Jew," *The Spectator*, January 22, 2005, pp. 18–19. Copyright © 2005 by *The Spectator*. Reproduced by permission of *The Spectator*.

by train. It was completely surrounded and subdivided by electric barbed-wire fencing. We saw pitiful starved figures in rags and many SS. We got out but had to leave our luggage on the train, never to see it again. Men and women had to line up separately and were sorted. The boys and the strong ones went into the camp. Everybody else who was sick or weak or over 45 years old (judged by appearance only) went straight into the gas chambers and was then cremated. All small children were also gassed, as they were of no use to the workforce.

She continued:

Our carriage had to line up separately.... There were 50 of us. Of these, six were called out by name, we three were among them. We were lined up with the young ones who went into the camp. The other 44 went to the gas chamber. Then we were led into a bath where we saw Papa for the last time.

After 18 days at Auschwitz, by some miracle, my mother and my grandmother were given the chance to volunteer for work at Belsen. It is an extraordinary fact that she is one of the few people able to say that, in some senses, Belsen was an improvement on Auschwitz. In the letter of 20 November 1945 she wrote, 'We did have a washroom and, although the water was icy cold, it did not have the foul smell, like in Auschwitz.'

These days she is less forthcoming. When I ask her for more information she clams up. Not long ago at her kitchen table I reduced her to tears with my repeated questions. 'Why are you doing this to me?' she pleaded. 'Why are you torturing me?' But I pressed on. The tears continued to flow and I could see all the loss in those tears, of her father, of her own childhood. I could see the dark depths of horror. 'Mum, this can be good for you—crying is good ... get it all out ... cry....' But my mother has never willingly talked about the camps, and she did not do so at the kitchen table—except to impart one infinitely forlorn piece of information. She tells who the 'Mickey' is in her collection of letters. It is my mother. She is Mickey. Her family sobriquet was 'Maus'. So 'Mickey' was 'Mickey Mouse'. And Mickey was liberated by the Americans!

Children of Survivors Need to Understand

Why was I torturing her? Was I torturing her? All I know is that the children of survivors need to make sense of their parents' suffering. I spend a little of each day, and sometimes a lot, either racked with guilt about my own conduct in today's society or with paranoia about what the present world might do to us.

'What would I have done?' I ask myself. 'What should I be doing now? What am I doing for those being persecuted today—among them the Palestinians, who are suffering at the hands of Jews? But for a turn of fate, could I have been a Nazi too? What unclean thoughts do I have about Islam and our Arab neighbours? What are my thoughts when I see devout Muslims on our streets in traditional dress, speaking poor English? Am I not looking at myself? Are they not just another separated community of black-coated Hasidic Jews? Did my people not look strange, separate and uncompromising in the central Europe of the 1930s?'

As for paranoia, I see Nazification in odd places, such as letters from the local council, EU [European Union] regulations, creeping state interference in our lives, the mania for control-freakery by corporations. I am a free-born, indeed a privileged, Englishman—raised in London, educated at Charterhouse—but part of me fully expects to be imprisoned at some stage in my life for something I haven't done. There is more than a bit of Kafka in all of us Jews. If it is a cold day, I force myself to imagine the feet that trod snow-covered Silesian roads on death marches, or the pain of a Polish winter and sleeping on a plank-bed in louse-ridden barracks of 700 souls. We Jews are not a fun lot.

Discovering Jewish Heritage

My own journey of discovery began late. I had no idea I was Jewish until I was 16. So deep did my parents bury their past that for many years I did not know that they had one, at least not one that was out of the ordinary. I remember a summer's day in my childhood when I saw my mother in a bathing suit and noticed for the first time the number on her arm. 'What is that?' I asked her. 'It is my number,' she said. I assumed that every mother had a number.

I was, and remain, a middle-of-the-road Anglican. My parents had me baptised at the parish church when I was six. I was married in the same church, and worship there to this day. It was a teacher—a historian and ex-interrogator of Nazis—who led me to the truth. He was assisting me with my written English, since I had a tendency to use strange, possibly Germanic, constructions; and his questions prompted me to question my parents. Not only was my mother a camp survivor, it turned out, but my father had fled to England from Austria in 1938, only to be arrested as an enemy alien after the outbreak of war. He was eventually sent to a camp in Australia, but he has never blamed the British for his treatment.

Since becoming a Jew, as it were, I have been reading around the subject. Paul Johnson's *A History of the Jews* (1987) is a good starting place. Martin Gilbert's 828-page *The Holocaust* (1986) takes courage. I do not think I will ever forget a paragraph in his preface describing a trip to Treblinka: 'I stepped down from the cart onto the sandy soil: a soil that was grey rather than brown. Driven by I know not what impulse, I ran my hand through that soil, again and again. The earth beneath my feet was coarse and sharp; filled with the fragments of human bone.'

Lasting Effects of the Holocaust

Then there is Isaac Bashevis Singer whose stories, translated from the Yiddish, recall the Jewish world in the Warsaw of the 1930s—the richness, the clatter and the colour of a people who no longer exist, in a language that is now all but dead. Visiting Poland today, you will still see the street names, Ulica Krochmalna or Marshalkowska, but you will not see the people who once lived and loved there, or find any record of their lives. Before the war, according to Paul Johnson's book, there were 3.5 million Jews living in Poland; today there are perhaps 5,000. What unimaginable cruelty is contained in those figures!

A Duty Not to Hate

As we prepare for the 60th anniversary of the liberation of Auschwitz, I am more than ever convinced that we Jews must excise hate. Of course, it is easy for one who has never suffered to talk about excising hate, but I nonetheless believe that I have a duty not to hate. It was hatred that caused the Holocaust.

When on 27 January I take my mother's arm—tattoo number A-25466—I will think not just of the crematoria and the cattle trucks but of Darfur, Rwanda, Zimbabwe, Jenin, Fallujah. I will pray that each of us who is born of suffering becomes also the end-post for it. If the survivors and their descendants do not lead the way, who will?

This little band of 600 has a terrible responsibility—to live well in the name of those who did not live and to discourage the building of walls and bulldozing of villages. Even more than this, they—and all Jews—need to be the voice of conscience that will prevent Israel from adopting the mantle of oppressor, and to reject the label 'anti-Semite' for those who speak out against Israel's policies in the occupied territories.

For those who went to the death camps were indeed lambs to the slaughter, but they very rarely lost their humanity. It was their very dignity against the worst that man can do to man, more than anything else, which commands the pity we have.

This is how my mother recalls the liberation of Salzwedel:

> At that time some Frenchmen were doing forced labour in the same factory and told us that the Americans were already very close. We could not believe it. We had waited so long for this day and had been so often disappointed that we no longer believed it possible. Then ... the first American tank arrived. There was indescribable rejoicing, shouting and crying; you just cannot imagine it. The SS were arrested; one tried to escape and was shot immediately.
>
> It was an almost unreal feeling to be free, to take a walk on one's own without the SS, without marching five in a row. We met a really nice German woman who looked after us with food, clothes etc.

My grandmother, who was liberated at the same time as my mother, lived in St John's Wood until the age of 94 and corresponded for the rest of her life with the German lady who had befriended her outside the gates of Salzwedel. They did not lose their humanity. Why should we?

A Visit to Auschwitz

Natalie Semotiuk

Natalie Semotiuk grew up in a comfortable home where war, murder, and suffering seemed far away and unreal. When she was sixteen, her family visited Auschwitz concentration camp. Being in one of the places where so many had died made the terror and injustice of the Holocaust more real to her. In this article, she talks about her feelings during that visit.

As a teenager living in a comfortable home, all I knew of terror was what I saw in movies and read in books. When I heard about war, ethnic cleansing, abuse of power, or even murders in my hometown, I felt disconnected. I didn't want to believe things so horrible really happened.

Last summer, my family visited Poland. When we planned a trip to Auschwitz, a World War II concentration camp, I knew I'd walk on ground where people had died. But until I got there, it didn't seem real to me.

When we got to Auschwitz, I saw a brick wall, electric fences, and a museum building. As we went in, I thought, Of course we're not going to see the real Auschwitz—it's just going to be another boring museum tour. A man stood in the corner, in front of two doors. He smiled and said, "Welcome to Auschwitz."

When we walked out of the museum, I was shocked to see the entire camp still intact. The entrance gate said, *"Arbeit Macht Frei,"* which means, "Work Shall Set You Free." I started shivering and didn't stop until after we left.

When we saw the kitchens where prisoners were fed one meal a day, I remembered a family friend who'd survived Auschwitz. He'd worked in the kitchen. Knowing that frightened me. It made it seem too real.

Natalie Semotiuk, "I Didn't Want to Know," *New Moon*, pp. 20–21. Copyright © 2004 by New Moon Publishing. Reproduced by permission. www.newmoongirls.com.

We saw the wall where people were shot and the solitary rooms where they were starved or suffocated. I thought, That's it! It's too much! I want to go home. But we weren't done yet. There was one place left, and I didn't want to see it.

The Gas Chambers

As it came into view, the ground seemed to fall away from my feet. This was the moment I dreaded most. Reluctantly, we entered the room where the Nazis killed over a million people with poisonous gas. Tears flowed down my cheeks. In the next room stood four open ovens where the bodies of the dead were burned. Flowers lay on one of the ovens. I wished I'd brought flowers. I wanted to comfort the people who'd died here and comfort myself. I wanted to scream, "I'm only 16—I shouldn't have to see this!" Then I thought of Anne Frank's famous diary. She was my age when she died here. I felt so weak compared to her.

I looked at my family's pale faces. We all stood in silence. I was filled with admiration for everyone who survived the camps, and I felt sympathy for those who didn't. I'll never forget that moment.

As we left, my father asked the tour guide why he worked at Auschwitz. He said he didn't want people to forget what happened.

Forgetting Auschwitz would insult every life lost there. The greatest weapon we have against tragedies like this is awareness. I know now that terror and injustice are real. But I also know we can stop them. To keep something like this from happening again, we must refuse to go along with prejudice and hatred.

Organizations to Contact

The editors have compiled the following list of organizations concerned with the issues debated in this book. The descriptions are derived from materials provided by the organizations. All have publications or information available for interested readers. The list was compiled on the date of publication of the present volume; the information provided here may change. Be aware that many organizations take several weeks or longer to respond to inquiries, so allow as much time as possible.

American-Israeli Cooperative Enterprise (AICE)
2810 Blaine Drive, Chevy Chase, MD 20815
(301) 565-3918 • fax: (301) 587-9056
e-mail: aiceresearch@gmail.com
Web site: www.jewishvirtuallibrary.org

The American-Israeli Cooperative Enterprise (AICE) was established in 1993 as a nonprofit, nonpartisan organization to strengthen the relationship between the United States and Israel by emphasizing the values that both nations share. AICE sponsors the Jewish Virtual Library, an online collection of information about Jewish history, Israel, American-Israeli relations, the Holocaust, anti-Semitism, and Judaism.

Anne Frank Center USA
38 Crosby Street, Fifth Floor, New York, NY 10013
(212) 431-7993 • fax: (212) 431-8375
e-mail: info@annefrank.com
Web site: www.annefrank.com

The Anne Frank Center USA is a not-for-profit organization that promotes the universal message of tolerance by providing information and educational materials about Anne Frank, the history of the Holocaust, and discrimination today, including a collection of downloadable study guides and related educational materials.

Anti-Defamation League
P.O. Box 96226, Washington, DC   20090-6226
Web site: www.adl.org

The Anti-Defamation League (ADL) fights anti-Semitism and all forms of bigotry in the United States and abroad through information, education, legislation, and advocacy. The organization's Web site has a section on the Holocaust, including a variety of articles and information on children of the Holocaust.

Facing History and Ourselves National Foundation (FHAO)
16 Hurd Road, Brookline, MA   02445-6919
(617) 232-1595 • Fax: (617) 232-0281
Web site: www.facinghistory.org

Since 1976, FHAO has been engaging students of diverse backgrounds in an examination of racism, prejudice, and anti-Semitism to promote the development of a more humane and informed citizenry. By studying the historical development and lessons of the Holocaust and other examples of genocide, students make the essential connection between history and the choices they confront in their own lives. In addition to offering online classes to educators and students, FHAO publishes resource books and study guides, including *Facing History and Ourselves: Holocaust and Human Behavior*.

The Holocaust History Project (THHP)
Web site: www.holocaust-history.org

The Holocaust History Project is a free archive of documents, photographs, recordings, and essays regarding the Holocaust, including direct refutation of Holocaust denial. Among the material on the site are essays about events and people, scientific and legal analyses, original Nazi documents, expert witness testimony, transcripts of many of the Nuremberg trials, and the complete texts of two seminal works, Jean-Claude Pressac's *Auschwitz* and Robert Jay Lifton's *The Nazi Doctors*. In addition, THHP volunteers personally answer e-mails from thousands of students each year.

Organizations to Contact

Holocaust Memorial Center (HMC)
28123 Orchard Lake Road, Farmington Hills, MI 48334-3738
(248) 553-2400 • fax: (248) 553-2433
e-mail: info@holocaustcenter.org
Web site: www.holocaustcenter.org

The original Holocaust Memorial Center (HMC) museum, the first institution of its kind in the United States, opened in 1981 in a suburb of Detroit, Michigan. It was the fulfillment of a dream of Rabbi Charles H. Rosenzveig, a Holocaust survivor. The current museum, opened in 2004, is a contemporary building that conveys the center's mission of remembrance and education. The center's Web site contains a virtual tour of the museum as well as a section of oral histories.

Holocaust Resource Center (HRC) of Kean University
Kean University Library, 2nd Floor, Union, NJ 07083
(908) 737-4660 • fax: (908) 737-4664
e-mail: keanhrc@kean.edu
Web site: www.kean.edu/~hrc

The HRC of Kean University opened its doors in the fall semester of 1982. The center is a joint initiative between the university and the Holocaust Resource Foundation, a private philanthropic organization. The center collects and disseminates knowledge of the Holocaust to commemorate and strengthen education about it. In addition, the center offers an annual free lecture series and a tuition-free graduate course for teachers called "Teaching the Holocaust."

Nizkor Project
e-mail: webmaster@nizkor.org
Web site: www.nizkor.org

The Nizkor Project is a Canadian nonprofit organization that provides material dealing with the phenomenon and history of hate, especially the Nazi Holocaust, material that documents and exposes such hate, and nonviolent methods and tools for combating it. *Nizkor* is a Hebrew word that means

"We will remember." The Web site includes information on concentration camps, people and places of the Holocaust, and the Nuremburg trials.

Prevent Genocide International (PGI)
1804 S Street NW, Washington, DC   20009
(202) 483-1948 • fax: (202) 328-0627
e-mail: info@preventgenocide.org
Web site: preventgenocide.org

PGI is a global education and action network established in 1998 with the purpose of bringing about the elimination of genocide. The foremost goal of Prevent Genocide International is to cultivate well-informed and articulate voices in many nations able to speak out in the emerging global civil society against the crime of genocide. PGI maintains a multilingual Web site, which includes a database of government documents and news releases, as well as original content provided by members.

Remember.org: A Cybrary of the Holocaust
P.O. Box 39, Augusta, GA   30903
(706) 736-2549
e-mail: jwkorn@remember.org
Web site: www.remember.org

Part of the Alliance for a Better Earth, Remember.org is an extensive collection of materials about the Holocaust contributed by visitors to the site. The site includes art; poetry; images; interviews with survivors, liberators, and others; a 360-degree virtual tour of the camps at Auschwitz-Birkenau; and other educational materials.

Simon Wiesenthal Center
1399 South Roxbury Drive, Los Angeles, CA   90035
(310) 553-9036 • fax: (310) 553-4521
e-mail: information@wiesenthal.net
Web site: www.wiesenthal.com

The Simon Wiesenthal Center is an international Jewish human rights organization. The center confronts anti-Semitism, hate and terrorism, promotes human rights and dignity, supports Israel, defends the safety of Jews worldwide, and teaches the lessons of the Holocaust for future generations. The center's Museum of Tolerance challenges visitors to confront bigotry and racism and to understand the Holocaust in both historic and contemporary contexts. The Museum of Tolerance also provides an online multimedia learning center with virtual exhibits and more than three thousand text files.

United States Holocaust Memorial Museum
100 Raoul Wallenberg Place, SW
Washington, DC 20024-2126
(202) 488-0400
e-mail: aabril@ushmm.org
Web site: www.ushmm.org

The goal of the United States Holocaust Museum is to document, study, and interpret Holocaust history, primarily that of the genocide during Nazi Germany from 1933–1945. By providing exhibits, maintaining lists of victims and survivors, and by providing a library and archives to visitors, the museum preserves the memories of the victims while provoking reflection on visitors' roles in preventing such actions again. The museum offers student and teacher resources on its Web site, as well as a series of online exhibitions.

University of Southern California Shoah Foundation Institute
Leavey Library, 650 West 35th Street, Suite 114
Los Angeles, CA 90089-2571
(213) 740-6001 • fax: (213) 740-6044
e-mail: vhi-acc@usc.edu
Web site: college.usc.edu/vhi

The USC Shoah Foundation Institute for Visual History and Education, with an archive of nearly 52,000 videotaped testimonies from Holocaust survivors and other witnesses, is part of the College of Letters, Arts and Sciences at the University of Southern California. The USC Shoah Foundation Institute works with a network of partners to provide educational services that reach educators, students, and the general public around the world. Some of the video testimonies are available online.

Voice/Vision Holocaust Survivor Oral History Archive
The University of Michigan-Dearborn, Mardigian Library
4901 Evergreen Road, Dearborn, MI 48128-1491
(313) 583-6300 • fax: (313) 593-5561
e-mail: holocaust@umd.umich.edu
Web site: holocaust.umd.umich.edu

Since 1981, Dr. Sidney Bolkosky, professor of history at the University of Michigan-Dearborn, has interviewed Holocaust survivors. The University's Mardigian Library has been the repository of these interviews. The purpose of the Voice/Vision Holocaust Survivor Oral History Archive is to maintain a collection of oral testimonies of those who survived the Holocaust and make them widely accessible for educational purposes. Many of the interviews are available on the organization's Web site.

Yad Vashem, The Holocaust Martyrs' and Heroes' Remembrance Authority
P.O.B. 3477, Jerusalem 91034
    Israel
Web site: www.yadvashem.org

Yad Vashem, the Holocaust Martyrs' and Heroes' Remembrance Authority, was established in 1953 by an act of the Israeli legislature, the Knesset. Since its inception, Yad Vashem has documented the history of the Jewish people during the Holocaust period, preserving the memory and story of each of the six million victims and imparting the legacy of the Holocaust for generations to come through its archives, library, school, and museums, as well as through recognition of the

Organizations to Contact

Righteous Among the Nations, those non-Jews who risked their lives to save Jews during the Holocaust. Yad Vashem is located on Har Hazikaron, the Mount of Remembrance, in Jerusalem.

For Further Research

Books

Anonymous, translated by Philip Boehm, *A Woman in Berlin: Eight Weeks in the Conquered City: A Diary*. New York: Metropolitan Books/Holt, 2005.

Mary Berg, *The Diary of Mary Berg: Growing up in the Warsaw Ghetto*. Oxford, England: Oneworld, 2006.

Doris L. Bergen, *War and Genocide: A Concise History of the Holocaust*. Lanham, MD: Rowman and Littlefield, 2003.

Corrie ten Boom and Elizabeth and John Sherrill, *The Hiding Place*. Grand Rapids, MI: Chosen Books, 2006.

Erin Einhorn, *The Pages In Between: A Holocaust Legacy of Two Families, One Home*. New York: Touchstone, 2008.

Ben Flanagan and Donald Bloxham, eds., *Remembering Belsen: Eyewitnesses Record the Liberation*. London: Vallentine Mitchell, 2005.

Anne Frank, *The Diary of a Young Girl*. New York: Bantam, 1997.

Saul Friedlander, *The Years of Extermination: Nazi Germany and the Jews, 1939–1945*. New York: Harper Perennial, 2008.

Etty Hillesum, *Etty Hillesum: An Interrupted Life: The Diaries, 1941–1943*. New York: Holt, 1996.

Bernice Lerner, *The Triumph of Wounded Souls: Seven Holocaust Survivors' Lives*. Notre Dame, IN: University of Notre Dame Press, 2004.

Primo Levi, *Survival in Auschwitz*. Minooka, IL: BN Publishing, 2007.

Daniel Mendelsohn, *The Lost: A Search for Six of Six Million*. New York: Harper Perennial, 2007.

Martin Schiller, *Bread, Butter and Sugar: A Boy's Journey Through the Holocaust and Postwar Europe*. Lanham, MD: Hamilton Books, 2007.

Mathilde Apelt Schmidt, *My Life on Two Continents*. New York: iUniverse, 2006.

H. Pierre Secher, ed. and trans., *Left Behind in Nazi Vienna: Letters of a Jewish Family Caught in the Holocaust, 1939–1941*. Jefferson, NC: McFarland, 2004.

Toby F. Sonneman, *Shared Sorrows: A Gypsy Family Remembers the Holocaust*. Hatfield: University of Hertfordshire Press, 2002.

Art Spiegelman, *The Complete Maus: A Survivor's Tale*. New York: Pantheon Books, 1996.

Michael Takiff, *Brave Men, Gentle Heroes: American Fathers and Sons in World War II and Vietnam*. New York: Morrow, 2003.

Elie Wiesel, *Night*, Revised. New York, Hill and Wang, 2006.

Walter Stanoski Winter, *Winter Time: Memoirs of a German Sinto Who Survived Auschwitz*. Hatfield, United Kingdom: University of Hertfordshire Press, 2004.

Periodicals

Benjamin Ferencz, "The Holocaust and the Nuremberg Trials," *UN Chronicle*, December 2005.

Deborah Hoffman, "Children of the Gulag," *Russian Life*, November–December 2007.

Junior Scholastic, "Children of the Holocaust: Two Young Survivors Tell About the Terrors of Nazi Camps," March 26, 2007.

Arthur Krystal, "My Holocaust Problem," *American Scholar*, Winter 2006.

William F.S. Miles, "Echoes of the Holocaust in a Parisian Suburb," *Contemporary Review*, Spring 2007.

Jack and Ina Polak, "Interview with Holocaust Survivors," *UN Chronicle*, March–May 2006.

John Ranz, "The Death March to Buchenwald," *Midstream*, November–December 2007.

Rob Salem, "Adolf Hitler: An Effective Leader?" *Hindsight*, September 2007.

Index

A

Ambushes, 53
Amen, John, 106, 108–110
American soldiers/army
    Flossenburg camp liberation, 76–77
    Göring's surrender to, 106
    Oberaltstadt camp liberation, 98–100
    Salzwedel camp liberation, 126
Anti-Semitic propaganda, 84
Arrests, 28, 30, 71, 75
Auschwitz-Birkenau concentration camp
    barrack housing, 38
    death pits, 33
    gas chamber sorting, 32–33, 35–36, 122
    gold teeth removal, 46–48
    identification tattoos, 36, 124
    inmate hierarchy, 33–34
    liberation from, 89–96
    as museum, 127–128
    smuggling in, 30

B

Barrack housing
    at Auschwitz, 38
    conditions of, 12–13, 17–19, 33–36
    elderly residents in, 20
    food issues in, 13, 19
    latrine in, 20–21
    quarantine to, 38–39
Begging for food, 70

Bergen-Belsen concentration camp, 72, 121
Birkenau. *See* Auschwitz-Birkenau concentration camp
Blockältester (barrack captain), 34, 39, 47
Blomberg, Werner von, 113
Body searches, 33
Bormann, Martin, 115
Bribery, 71
Bunker massacre, 72

C

Children of survivors
    hate and, 125–126
    Hitler's influence on, 118–120
    Jewish heritage of, 124–125
    lessons learned by, 123–124
Chloral hydrate use, 67
Cohen, Leon, 38–49
Cohn, Martha, 51–61
Cologne Jews, 83
Concentration camps
    American liberation of, 76–77
    Bergen-Belsen, 72, 121
    crematoriums, 32–33, 75–76
    emotional consequences of, 19
    evacuation of, 76
    Flossenburg, 74–76
    Göring, Herman and, 115–116
    Jews in, 12–13, 86
    as museums, 13–14
    Plaszow, 30
    Polish Jews and, 119
    Salzwedel, 126
    Terezín, 16–22

Treblinka, 124
work/employment issues, 29, 34, 38–49, 75, 122
See also Auschwitz-Birkenau concentration camp

Concentration camps, liberation from
Auschwitz, 89–96
Flossenburg, 76–77
food issues, 90–91, 93, 96, 98–99
Nuremburg Trials, 106–116
Oberaltstadt, 97–105
See also Oberaltstadt camp liberation

Concentration camps, life outside
Christian assistance, 70–77
deportation assistance, 66–69
forging documents, 62–65
Hitler Youth Organization and, 78–87
spying on, 51–61

Convoys, 52–53
Corpse layering in crematoriums, 41
Corrosive liquid disinfectant, 32
Crematoriums
in concentration camps, 32–33, 75–76
corpse layering in, 41
furnaces, 47–48
layout of, 42
memories of, 94
Czech Republic, 18, 101

D

Death camps. *See* Concentration camps
Death pits, 33
Deportation
children *vs.* parents, 67
to concentration camps, 12
document forging and, 63
refugee rescues from, 69
by train, 68
Displaced persons (DP) camps, 100

E

Eighteenth SS Armee Korps, 52
Einschieben order, 48
Elderly ghetto residents, 20
Emotional consequences
of being Sonderkommandos, 45–46
of concentration camps, 19
See also Children of survivors
European Union, 123
Evacuation of concentration camps, 76
Extermination camps. *See* Concentration camps

F

Family searches, 100–102, 104–105
Flossenburg concentration camp, 74–76
Food issues
after liberation, 90–91, 93, 96, 98–99
in barracks, 13, 19
begging for, 70
inmate rations, 35
smuggling, 24–27, 71
trading for, 25
Forging documents, 62–65
Freeman, Helen, 97–105
Freeman, Joseph, 97–105
Friesová, Jana Renée, 16–22

Index

Fritsch, Werner von, 113–114
Furnaces, 47–48

G

Gas chambers
  layout of, 44–45
  as museum, 128
  rumors of, 82
  sorting for, 32–33, 35–36, 122
  undressing halls, 42
  use of, 13
  victim questions about, 43–44
Gender separation in concentration camps, 31
Gestapo (German secret police), 111, 112
Ghetto life
  commercial contact within, 70
  description of, 12
  for elderly residents, 20
  entry passes, 71
  marriage and, 28–29
  moving into, 21–22
  for Polish Jews, 72–73
  smuggling and, 23–30
  work issues, 24
Gilbert, Martin, 124
Goeth, Amon, 30
Gold teeth removal, 46–48, 75
Göring, Herman
  behavior problems with, 110–111
  capture of, 106–107
  concentration camps and, 115–116
  description of, 111–113
  duping the populace, 114–115
  pretrial interrogations, 108–109
  as War Minister, 113–114
Greenspan, Henry, 89–96

Grief, Gideon, 38–49
Grünfeld, Benny, 31–37

H

Hasidic Jews, 123
Heyman, Walter, 62–65
Himmler, Heinrich, 113, 115–116
Hindenburg, Paul von, 112
A History of the Jews (Johnson), 124
Hitler, Adolf
  as armed forces commander, 114
  concentration camps and, 115–116
  leadership issues of, 112–113
  Nazi Party leader, 12, 59
  propaganda images of, 84–85
  resentment against, 118–120
Hitler Youth Organization
  Jewish relations, 80–83, 83–86
  joining, 80
  post-war information, 86–87
Holden, Wendy, 51–61
Holocaust defined, 12
The Holocaust (Gilbert), 124
Holocaust Memorial Day (January 27), 121
Holocaust Memorial Museum, 120
Hospitalization of refugees, 91–92

I

Identification tattoos
  after liberation, 86, 95
  engraving, 36, 38
  shame over, 20, 124, 125
Infanticide, 81–82, 122
Inmate hierarchy, 33–34

141

J

Jewish Council, 21
Jewish heritage, 124–125
Johnson, Eric A., 78–87
Johnson, Paul, 124, 125

K

Kraków, Poland, 24, 27
Kristallnacht (November 7, 1983), 83–86
Kutschera, Franz ("Butcher of Warsaw"), 73

L

Lambert, Raymond-Raoul, 66–69
Latrine conditions, 20–21
Lehar, Franz, 116
Lessons learned from Holocaust, 123–124
Levy, Shirley Paryzer, 118–120
Liberation. *See* Concentration camps, liberation
Lipmann, Anthony, 121–126
Luftwaffe (German air force), 107
Lukas, Richard C., 70–77
Lutz, Hubert, 78–87

M

Marriage in the ghetto, 28–29
Milch, Erhard, 112
Milles Camp deportation center, 66
Mladá Boleslav, Czech Republic, 18
Muslims, 123

N

National Socialist German Workers' Party (Nazis), 12, 79
Nineteenth German Army, 52
Nordstern, Hubert, 80–81
Nuremberg Laws, 107
Nuremburg Trials, 106–116

O

Oberaltstadt camp liberation
  Americans' arrival into, 98–100
  disappointment after, 102–103
  hope after, 103–104
  by Russians, 97–98
  searching for family, 100–102, 104–105

P

Palestinians, 123
Plaszow concentration camp, 30
Plotkin, Diane, 23–30
Polish Jews, 72–73, 119
Polish Underground, 75
Pretrial interrogations, Nuremburg Trials, 108–109
Prisoner-of-war camp, 92

Q

Quarantine barracks, 38–39

R

Rebuilding life after liberation, 92–93
Reflections on the Holocaust (Wiesel), 13

Index

Refugee rescues, 69
Religious issues
  by children of survivors, 123
  Christian aid, 70–77
  Jewish spirituality, 62–63
  in pre-war Poland, 105–106
Reuband, Karl-Heinz, 78–87
Ribbentrop, Joachim von, 115
Richthofen, Manfred von ("Red Baron"), 107
Roadblocks during war, 57–58
Röhm, Ernst, 113
Rubin, Agi, 89–96
Russian liberation, 94–95

S

Salzwedel concentration camp, 126
Schiff, William J., 23–30
Schönhaus, Cioma, 62–65
Semotiuk, Natalie, 127–128
Singer, Isaac Bashevis, 125
Skarzsysko labor camp, 30
Smuggling
  food, 24–27, 71
  metal bits, 29–30
Sonderkommandos, 38–49
Sonnemann, Emmy, 112
Sonnenfeldt, Richard W., 106–116
Spying against Germans
  ambush intelligence, 53
  avoiding roadblocks, 57–58
  carrying messages, 54, 60–61
  escaping detection, 54–57
  meeting contacts, 58–60
  meeting convoys, 52–53
  spinning falsehoods, 51–52
Stubendienst (barrack assistants), 34
Stürmer (magazine), 84

T

Tattoos. *See* Identification tattoos
Terezín concentration camp, 16–22
Trading for food, 25
Train deportations, 68
Treaty of Versailles, 107
Treblinka concentration camp, 124
Typhoid fever, 86

U

Undressing halls in concentration camps, 42

V

Versailles, Treaty of, 107

W

Warsaw Uprising, 73–74
Wehrmacht (german armed forces), 29, 62, 89
Wiesel, Elie, 13
Work/employment
  after liberation, 90, 119
  body searches, 33
  in concentration camps, 29, 34, 38–49, 75, 122
  forging documents, 62–65
  lack of in ghettos, 24
  in Nazi Party, 79
  sickness and, 13
  smuggling, 24–25
  spying, 51–61
Wos, Paul Zenon, 70–77
Wunder waffen (wonder weapons), 53

940.5318 Hol
The Holocaust